FREE MONEY
The Gambler's Quest

Declan Lynch

TRANSWORLD IRELAND

TRANSWORLD IRELAND
an imprint of The Random House Group Limited
20 Vauxhall Bridge Road, London SW1V 2SA
www.rbooks.co.uk

First published in 2009 by Transworld Ireland
a division of Transworld Publishers Ltd

A CIP catalogue record for this book
is available from the British Library.

ISBN 9781848270305

Extract on page 206 from 'Chinese all-stars spread their wings but
home dynasty remains in place' by Will Buckley, published in the *Guardian*
16 August 2008 © Guardian News & Media Ltd 2008.
Extracts on page 89 from 'Flash Harry: the outrageous world of Britain's
premier punter' by Chris McGrath, published in the *Independent*
10 March 2008 © The Independent 2008.

Addresses for Random House Group Ltd companies outside the UK
can be found at: www.randomhouse.co.uk
The Random House Group Ltd Reg. No. 954009

The Random House Group Limited supports The Forest Stewardship Council (FSC),
the leading international forest-certification organization. All our titles that are
printed on Greenpeace-approved FSC-certified paper carry the FSC logo.
Our paper procurement policy can be found at
www.rbooks.co.uk/environment

If you can make one heap of all your winnings
And risk it on one turn of pitch-and-toss,
And lose, and start again at your beginnings
And never breathe a word about your loss . . .

. . . you'll be a man, my son!

From 'If', Rudyard Kipling

Prologue

Two things got me going on this gambling craze.

It started with the opening of a branch of Paddy Power in Rathfarnham village, close to where I lived. A mundane event, you would think, in a country that was becoming rich. Except it was only a few doors away from a branch of Ladbrokes, which had been there for many years.

It seemed that there would be a fight to the finish between the two of them, that the villagers would have to choose between Ladbrokes and Paddy Power, that only one betting office could survive on this suburban street.

Sure enough, there was soon a decisive move – another betting office opened, a branch of Boylesports.

And then we moved from Rathfarnham to County Wicklow, about a mile outside Avoca, which was far enough from the one betting office in the village to persuade me that I needed to open an internet betting account.

Not that I had been making daily visits to the bookies when I lived in Dublin, or even weekly visits, but I guess the idea of internet betting helped me to adjust to the idea of country living – how could anyone feel isolated from his fellow man when he could get hooked up to the international leisure industry in this way?

I had been doing some internet betting by proxy, getting a friend who was already hooked up to throw the odd tenner on a televised football match for me. To have 'an interest'. But you need to do it yourself to fully appreciate the sublime beauty of it, the fatal beauty of it. Even now, three years after I opened my account, I have not lost my sense of wonder that something so brilliant and so potentially catastrophic can be available in his own home to every man who can get himself an internet connection and a credit card.

They're sucking in the women too, and we'll be looking at that.

They're sucking in the kids who already have an instinctive attachment to the internet, and who would quickly understand how well it works, how the net might have been made for gambling, with everything else thrown in just for luck.

They're sucking in everyone, because as the German-born Arabic scholar Franz Rosenthal put it, 'the subject of gambling is all-encompassing. It combines man's natural play instinct with his desire to know about his fate and his future.'

It is all-encompassing, although sports betting, which mainly concerns us here, is largely a male pursuit. And though the vast majority of gamblers fail to make any money at it, I have found that they tend to be men of above average intelligence – indeed it is often their very smartness which keeps them going, keeps them believing in their ability to make it pay.

But there may be no such thing as a typical gambler, because the instinct is so fundamental it is possessed by everyone to some degree.

There is a reality-challenging dissidence in most of us, a desire to turn life in our favour, rather than merely let things happen to us. Then there are the aficionados who make this the main purpose of their lives rather than an occasional indulgence. Every day they want to play God.

Which may help to explain why the great religions are so trenchantly opposed to gambling, especially Islam, which, perhaps uniquely among the world's major belief-systems, is still taken seriously by its adherents – in Ireland, Catholic priests can be heard giving tips for Cheltenham from the altar, which they shouldn't be doing. In theory.

So it was the sweet science of internet betting, allied to the general gambling boom that was filling the main street of Rathfarnham and every other town in Ireland with betting offices, which got me going on this.

I look at the modern betting offices with their banks of screens, like a stock exchange for people with no money; I look at the symbiotic relationship between internet betting and televised sport, and part of me rejoices, and part of me feels like old John Reith, founding father of the BBC, as he contemplated the masses indulging in the easy pleasures of television, 'a potential social menace of the first magnitude'.

With internet betting, perhaps not since those early days of television itself has the addictive personality been fed so seductively.

All forms of betting have become socially acceptable in this generation, but the sort you can do in the middle of the night on the laptop in your bedroom has a special kick.

Even without the new technology, gambling may well be the strongest of all the addictions, because the 'drug' is self-generated, it is not something you drink or smoke or snort. With the technology, an addiction that is already immensely powerful has been cranked up again, so that the addicted gambler sitting up late with the American football, betting on the Indianapolis Colts on the internet, is like the alcoholic who finds that he can drink at home while somehow replicating exactly the atmosphere of a great old pub. With a band playing.

You are alone, but you are not alone. As an internet punter you are part of something much bigger than yourself.

It is banned in America, France, Germany and Holland, but it is rampant all across this sporting world, and I believe that these days of unrestricted online betting may eventually be viewed the way we now view those wild years of promiscuity which were ended by Aids. In this analysis, online betting is the gambling equivalent of unprotected sex. There will be a lot of fun, and there will be a lot of destruction. And like that mental image that we still have of free-form romping in the LA bathhouses of the 1970s, it seems almost absurdly easy.

You google the website of any major betting organization you can think of, and there it is, a page full of possibilities. They are offering you markets on the traditional earners such as horse racing and the dogs, and if there is not enough horse racing and dog racing going on for you, there is now Virtual horse racing and Virtual dog racing too.

But there is also a long list of other sports to get your attention – in alphabetical order, depending on what is in season, you could be looking at Aussie Rules, American football, baseball, basketball, boxing, cricket, cycling, darts, football, Gaelic sports, golf, handball, hurling, motor racing, politics, rugby league, rugby union, snooker, tennis, volleyball – indeed, anything you have ever heard of that could vaguely be called sport, and some things you have probably never heard of, such as Futsal.

What is Futsal? Apparently it's a form of indoor football but that's not important. The important thing is that from time to time it's on TV, on Eurosport in the afternoon, and that there's usually a winner and a loser and therefore there is money to be made, or not as the case may be.

And in the ultimate manifestation of this marriage between betting and television, there is the Red Button on Sky, which connects you to the action in every sense. You could be watching a match between Manchester City and Aston Villa, and listening to the Skybet commentators analysing the match entirely in betting terms – City look a good bet at Evens to get the next corner kick . . . Villa have five players on yellow cards and the game is getting a bit tasty, that 3/1 on Villa to have a man sent off looks like the value . . . the possibilities are infinite, and once you are signed up to Skybet – it is not hard – you can use your remote control to bet on any of these exciting propositions, and they put whatever happens next on to your Sky bill.

And if for a few moments there is no competitive sport going on anywhere in the world, you can invest online in politics or in showbusiness – you may have noted that in the list of sports above, I put 'politics' between motor racing and rugby league. This was not a wry intervention on my part, it is a direct transcription of the menu on my betting website.

For the punter a general election or a series of *Strictly Come Dancing* or the last race at Ballinrobe ultimately amounts to the same thing: you win some, you lose some.

You could be under the duvet in Shinrone, County Offaly, having a bet on Barack Obama to win the great state of Florida, and then you could watch the results coming in on Sky News and CNN and Fox, staying up all night for the boxes to be opened in Tallahassee.

Yes, the world is the best that it has ever been.

They are offering you markets on events which are currently in progress, and events which are happening next week, and next year. They are offering you odds on what colour hat the Queen will be wearing at Royal Ascot, and who will be the next manager of Plymouth Argyle.

And while card games and casino-style gambling do not concern us here, they are also part of the service.

If you have even the smallest urge to gamble, in any way, in any place, at any time, you are, as they say, made up.

And maybe a lot of folks can pick it up and leave it down again, regarding it as no more than an amusement, like buying a lottery ticket once every few months; but I strongly suspect – and the record backs this up – that an increasing number of folks are finding it hard to leave it down, hard to take themselves away from something which, in these tough times, to quote George Bernard Shaw in *Man and Superman*, 'promises the poor what property performs for the rich, something for nothing'.

If you do this right, you might never have to work again.

You follow the instructions on how to open an account. It is not difficult. You type in the amount you want to deposit, and your password, and the last three numbers on the security strip of your credit card, and there it is, gone.

'Deposit Successful', it says. Straight away, the money is credited to your account and you can start betting.

'Bet Now', it says, beside every market you peruse. Or maybe 'Submit', which betimes feels more chillingly appropriate.

Entering these transactions, you can feel a bit like a stockbroker, the guys you see on the news when the Dow collapses, concentrating fiercely on their computer screens, apparently directing the affairs of the world. Those guys are gambling too, in fact the whole of the human race seems to be gambling in some shape or form, as we embark on this journey.

On the way, I believe that we will learn something about the nature of gambling in general and why it has such a powerful hold on us, particularly on men, millions of whom now relate to the world almost entirely through this link between gambling, TV and the internet, this devastatingly powerful three-way combination.

I figure the best way to do this is through a personal betting journal and various biographical reminiscences which naturally raise all these matters, which move from contemplation of the state of my internet account, to moments of sober reflection on the state of the world, in this the Age of Addiction.

I believe this is the only way I can do it, because I'm not good enough at gambling to write one of those 'how to' books which have served the public so well until now – *How to Win at Canasta*, and so on.

I also believe that two of the most challenging phenomena of our time are radical Islam and internet gambling.

And I know which side I'm on.

Of course I am not like the others.

My main purpose here is to write about gambling, which is not the same thing as gambling and then writing about it. I haven't made or lost a fortune, like the celebrity gambler writing his autobiography, telling the talk-show host that he was blind and now he can see.

But then I guess that even the Arsenal and England footballer Paul Merson, old 'Merse' himself, when he started going down, thought that he was not like the others, with their unexamined gambling lives. In fact a lot of men go down precisely because they think they are not like the others.

But they are.

25 January 2008

Deposit: 100 euro

I am opening this account on the day after it was learned that a Frenchman called Jérôme Kerviel, an employee of Société Générale, lost approximately five billion euros gambling on the stock exchange. It was five billion euros of other people's money, but it was still five billion euros.

Which is a lot for one man to lose.

So on this day of all days, as I place 100 euros in my internet betting account, to keep us going, I feel like a sober and responsible citizen. I feel like some guy putting a few bob into the Credit Union for his daughter's education.

Indeed, as I start this quest I feel like that mythical character who lands in New York with 100 dollars, aiming to make his fortune.

I think all gamblers are in love with the idea that mighty oaks from little acorns grow. Even if a lot of little acorns have already been planted, from which no oak has grown.

We know it can be done, and that is all that matters.

Yet there is always a frisson of self-doubt when you make any sort of deposit in your internet account, which in my case is with Blue Square, who say they are based in Alderney.

And it's only 100, after all, it's no more than that poor unfortunate character would have in his fist, as he landed in the New World with a head full of crazy dreams.

But for me, there's a bit of 'previous' to consider. About twelve years ago I gave up drinking, 'while it was still my idea', to quote Billy Connolly.

And I can honestly say that I have no desire to start drinking again.

At least not today.

And probably not tomorrow either.

But it provides, shall we say, a context. And in that context there are some watchful souls who would advise me in the strongest possible terms that I should not be venturing into other areas of addiction, under any circumstances.

Because it is such things that make men mad . . .

So while the layman might indeed regard this deposit of 100 as a sporting wager with no implications of a sinister kind for the state of my soul, or anyone else's soul, this 100 is still a number which would get them going in the great houses of addiction-treatment.

In there they insist that with gambling, as with drinking, the problem is not necessarily one of quantity, that you don't need to drink as much as Errol Flynn or gamble as much as Jérôme Kerviel to be called an addict. In fact they're lowering the bar all the time, in a way that seems to me not entirely devoid of self-interest.

So while it is twelve years since I stopped drinking, and nine since I stopped smoking, even after all that time you wouldn't want to be telling them in a group therapy room that you're embarking on a 'quest', that you're following the money wherever it takes you, in order to illuminate various aspects of the global gambling phenomenon.

'How do you feel about that?' they would say in the darkest tone, before telling you what they feel about it, in the strongest possible terms.

How do I feel about it?

I'll tell you in the autumn, when this punter's journey ends at the Ryder Cup, at Valhalla. And life being what it is, if that 100 has grown significantly, I will probably be happy, and if it goes the other way, I will probably be sad.

But at the outset I can say that I am quietly confident. You always feel that surge of hope at the start of a new betting campaign, even if every previous campaign has ultimately ended in defeat. With each fresh start, each successful deposit, you feel that you have accumulated so much wisdom, you are bound to get ahead this time, and stay ahead.

Sceptics will argue that you weren't accumulating wisdom, you were just accumulating losses, and the only wisdom to be gleaned is that you will lose again and again and again, until you stop.

But I don't want to stop. I enjoy this thing, and anyway my losses, such as they are, have never amounted to much. And I think that over the course of last year I may actually have broken even. And in the light of Damon Runyon's dictum that all of life is 6 to 4 against, that's as good as winning.

But there's a feeling of fear too, which never leaves you if you have done some work in the area of addiction.

And yet I believe it is a healthy fear. In fact I believe that this healthy fear makes me a better punter, a deeply conservative punter indeed, who will spurn almost anything bigger than Evens, in order to take the profit regardless of how small it may be, just to get ahead and stay ahead.

Not that this is all about me.

To begin, I'll break into the perfect 100 and have 70 at 2/7 on South Africa to win the One Day International against the West Indies, which is live on Sky Sports.

Let us go, then, on this journey that will end in Valhalla.

And may God help us all.

29 January 2008

♏   70 on South Africa to beat West Indies @ 2/7 – **Win***

☉   20 on Chelsea to beat Wigan @ 1/2 – **Win**

●   70 on Djokovic to beat Tsonga @ 4/11 – **Win**

🏌   15 on Cink to be 2nd to Woods – **Lose**

●   55 on Hartfield to beat Zabaleta @ 5/6 – **Win**

. . . +85**

I should state here that I do not intend to provide an intimate description of what happened in every sporting contest in which I have an interest between now and September, but in these early days it feels appropriate to go into some detail. †To get a feel for 'how it works', as they say in AA.

And I'm ahead already, so there is deep pleasure in the recollection. There will be times when it will not feel appropriate, when I'll simply want to forget. But this is not one of them.

Because after a weekend of good, honest, workmanlike punting, I am 85 euros ahead. That opening bet on the South African cricketers encapsulated certain aspects of my philosophy.

Clearly by staking 70 of the 100, I was risking the lion's share of my wad in the first skirmish of the campaign. But as the odds of 2/7 suggested, there was good reason to be confident in the result. So there was a certain level of risk here, but there was also a high probability of success. And at the core of my philosophy is this idea that a short-priced winner is always better than a big-priced loser. A gain of 20 on an outlay of 70 is more

---

*All stakes are rounded to the nearest 5 euros.
**All these figures represent overall (accumulated) profit or loss.
†You'll also find a glossary on page 241 for an explanation of any unfamiliar terminology

enjoyable in the end than a deficit of 20 on an outlay of 10. Just try it, and you'll see that I speak the truth.

But while this was a relatively relaxed encounter, with South Africa getting ahead and staying ahead, I would chide myself for having any bet on the basis that the event is being televised, and therefore the experience will be more enjoyable. The fact that something is on television is entirely irrelevant to the question of who wins and who loses. So if you are influenced in any way by your base desire for TV entertainment, you are giving a vital edge to the bookie. Unlike him, you are not devoting all your powers of concentration to the bottom line, because you are surrendering to the synergy between live TV sport and internet gambling, this wondrous development in the ascent of Man, on which I will muse much in the days and weeks to come.

So it is no accident that the bookies feverishly promote events that are shown live on TV, because they know that this automatically impairs the punter's judgement – or at least it causes him to consider things which should have no part in his calculations – again, no one ever won a bet 'because it was on the telly'.

Anyway, with my profit of 20, I made an in-depth study of the markets on the FA Cup fourth round, and I reasoned that Chelsea at 1/2 to beat Wigan had the distinct smell of free money about it. And I reasoned right, adding a tenner to my account. And as a bonus, the match was on live TV, though I hadn't known this when I made my investment – a happy accident which became happier still when I saw that Blue Square was offering a free bet of £20 sterling or 28 euros if you had a bet on any market in the Cup, and if Havant & Waterlooville scored against Liverpool at Anfield – and I fancied that Havant & Waterlooville might just score against Liverpool at Anfield. Lo and behold, H&W scored – twice – so I looked forward to my first free bet since the day I opened my first Blue Square account, which was the day of the Eurovision Song Contest of 2006 as I recall.

The reason I recall it is that I had my free bet of £25 on Brian Kennedy winning the Contest for Ireland, at odds of 33/1. Oh, how I laugh when I think about it now, when I contemplate my foolishness in the face of this powerful new magic I had found.

Yes, it is a form of magic that a punter such as I, who had been punting in the old-fashioned way since I was a child, had suddenly discovered that there was a better way, a much, much better way. A way that didn't involve you leaving the house, or even leaving your bed if you didn't fancy it. A way that didn't require you to stand shoulder to shoulder with a bunch of men in a state of high anxiety in a horrible betting office, handing real cash money across the counter, and not getting it back.

The day is gone when a move to a remote location could take a man away from his recreations, as Jeffrey Bernard discovered when he moved with his then wife to rural England, partly, it was thought, to stop him drinking – the nearest pub was in the village, six miles away. Undaunted, Bernard would post a letter to himself, and wait for the postman's van to deliver the letter. He would then get a lift back to the village in the van, go to the pub, and start drinking.

Even today, you might still need to do this if you really insist on doing your drinking in a pub. But if you just want to bet, you need never leave the house again.

High on the improbability of it all, using my Visa card I followed the simple instructions and lodged 50 euros with Blue Square, noting for the first time of many that my deposit was successful.

'Deposit Successful', it said, giving me the impression that I was already a winner, and I hadn't even started betting.

Then, still high on the improbability of it all, I had the 'value' bet on Brian Kennedy. Hell, I thought, it's free money anyway, this free bet of £20 or £25 with which all internet betting providers inveigle their clients into the realm of endless possibility.

Though I didn't choose Blue Square over Paddy Power because Blue Square was offering a slightly bigger free bet. I chose Blue Square because I prefer the colour blue to the colour green of Paddy Power. It seems easier on the eye.

Anyway, I threw away that first free bet on a load of nonsense. So on this occasion I steeled myself to take full advantage of a bookie's moment of weakness. We punters are forever being caught in moments of weakness, but bookies are made of different stuff. Clearly the wizards didn't imagine for a moment that Havant would score, and rightly so. But they did, and over the next forty-eight hours the wizards would take the hit.

In passing, I assume there's a reason why it takes up to forty-eight hours for the free bet to arrive in your account, a thought which struck me as I placed 70 of my own money on Novak Djokovic to beat Jo Wilfried Tsonga in the final of the Australian Open at odds of 4/11. 'Djoko', I felt, was 'a good thing' here. And after dropping the first set, he recovered like a man to fulfil his destiny, to take his first Grand Slam title, garnering another few millions for himself, and a handy 25 for me.

Still using my own money (we are perhaps now understanding why the free money takes forty-eight hours to kick in) I made the mistake of having 15 on Stewart Cink at 10/11 to finish second to Tiger Woods in the Buick, live on Setanta. A schoolboy error here, a bet placed out of boredom. Bookies don't price up these events out of boredom, so we shouldn't be showing our human weakness in this way.

But we do, especially when we're ahead, and feeling a bit gung-ho. Indeed I say I was betting with my own money but when you're ahead you feel like you're betting with the bookies' money, and this too leads to a certain level of irrational exuberance, which leads to errors of judgement.

Ah we are weak, we are so weak, and they are strong.

They know that it's a long day, that punters get bored, and that boredom will usually lead us astray. In fact, amid all the psychobabble, I believe that the role of boredom in every area of addiction is greatly underestimated – especially for men, who have little interest in going for long walks, who seem to need something with a shot of adrenalin to get them through the empty hours. The internet has clarified our thinking on the subject of boredom, by demonstrating that if they have the option, humans will often reject the robust attractions of 'real life', choosing instead to google away the time.

It can look worse than it actually is.

I might visit my Blue Square account several times a day, but most of the time I'm only passing through. I tend to be welded to the laptop anyway, with my writing, so in vacant or in pensive mood I might find myself checking out the Blue Square racing results service, for no good reason. Or maybe just to confirm that another 33/1 shot has won at Southwell, and to thank God that it's nothing to do with me.

Or maybe just to visit my money.

Now just 40 ahead, the free bet finally arrived and I studied the markets with a terrible intensity. I was most tempted by a tennis match in Chile between Zabaleta and Hartfield, both priced at 5/6. On paper, you'd fancy Zabaleta, because he's called Zabaleta, after all, and in the game of life, in Chile a Zabaleta will tend to beat a Hartfield. But drawing on my hard-won knowledge of the international tennis circuit, I was aware that Hartfield was no dozer. He had been slaughtered by Federer at the Australian Open recently, but unlike Zabaleta at least he was good enough to be there to get slaughtered.

Then I had a bit of luck. In attempting to have the free bet on Hartfield, I found the instructions too confusing, as I was probably meant to do, and ended up using my own money. Taking this as an omen, I put the free money on Hartfield too, who won in straight sets, resulting in a combined profit of roughly 45 euros.

So I am 85 ahead as I embark on this quest, and while this mightn't mean much in a world which contains men like Jérôme Kerviel, it represents a profit of 85 per cent on the initial investment, which at current interest rates is a hell of a lot more than you'll be getting from the Bradford & Bingley.

Now I must forge ahead. And with my deep knowledge of African football I would be tempted by Ivory Coast v Mali in the Africa Cup of Nations this evening, except there's been a lot of dark talk of match-fixing in relation to this tournament, and that, along with the involvement of the usual witch doctors and ju-ju merchants, is making me nervous. Clearly there are men who are not prepared to rely simply on their judgement in order to turn a profit. And I've got enough ju-ju of my own going on here.

I'll leave them to it, as I seek to consolidate with 70 on the Arsenal at 2/7 to beat Newcastle at home.

A MOMENT OF SOBER REFLECTION
UNUSUAL BETTING PATTERNS

IN AUGUST 2007, in the second round of the Orange Prokom Open in Sopot, a seaside resort in Poland, there was a tennis match.

And in the course of this tennis match, Betfair noted what appeared to be unusual betting patterns. So unusual, in fact, that initially Betfair refused to pay out on the winner. A full independent investigation was mounted by the tennis authorities which cleared the players of any wrongdoing.

It was reported that Betfair took about $7 million on the result of this match, but that does not concern us here.

For us, the one outstanding, almost overwhelming insight to be gleaned here came from the news that $7 million is reportedly ten times the usual volume of business on such an event.

Which means that Betfair would not be at all surprised to see $700,000 being wagered on the result of a tennis match in the second round of a small tournament in Poland.

That's 700 grand on one match, on one website.

Let us pause . . .

4 February 2008

- ⚽ 70 on Arsenal to beat Newcastle @ 2/7 – **Win**
- ⚽ 75 on Man Utd to beat Portsmouth @ 1/4 – **Win**
- 🏌 30 on Howell III in three-ball @ 5/4 – **Lose**
- 🏌 60 on Mickelson in three-ball @ 4/6 – **Win**
- 🏌 70 on Woods to win Dubai Desert Classic @ 2/7 in-running – **Win**
- ⚽ 45 on Ivory Coast to beat Guinea @ 4/9 – **Win**

. . . +170

With the Arsenal duly obliging and Man Utd adding another 20 to my account by beating Portsmouth at home, I have had six winners so far, and just one loser. This neatly illustrates one of my core beliefs.

It seems to me that picking winners is not necessarily the problem in betting. Indeed the average punter might well be astonished to discover that in a lifetime of punting, he might pick nearly as many winners as your JP McManus. Unfortunately, he just doesn't have the right amount of money on them.

A statement of the bleeding obvious, perhaps? No, I think it falls into another category, of things that are so obvious we don't notice them at all.

In these early exchanges, despite an almost unblemished record in terms of winners and losers, I have already displayed my weakness in this department. Yes, I now have a profit margin of 170 per cent. But somehow, unlike the professionals, I have not yet honed my instincts in such a way that I can reap the most extravagant rewards from my success.

Obviously, if I'd started out with 10,000, betting at the

equivalent rate, I would now have 27,000 in my account. Which would be nice.

But doing the maths is one thing; actually doing the business involves emotions which are alien to most people. Because most people, for some reason, are afraid of losing that original ten grand. They imagine that if the results went the wrong way, and they were down ten grand instead of up ten grand, they would be very unhappy.

Somehow, the giants of this game are not afraid of such things.

I sometimes wonder whether I would be so fearless if I were a single man with no responsibilities. But I was that soldier for a long time too, and even then I had these strange misgivings about losing ten grand on the proverbial throw of the dice. In fact I can't remember a time when I wasn't afraid of losing ten grand.

I still shudder when I hear of men winning large amounts for large amounts staked, because I know that if you're in the habit of betting ten grand at the one sitting, in the long run you'll almost certainly go down. And you will go down big, whereas all the regular punters with their fear and their self-loathing will go down small.

JP McManus didn't go down big. In fact he didn't go down at all. And at the rate I'm going, JP would probably have made about 270 grand, due to his genius for maximizing his positions. But the whole point of JP is that there are not many JPs knocking around. He may not be totally unique in being so far ahead of the posse, but he is still a member of an extremely rare species. We look at him the way we look at some odd bird, trying to decipher the source of his inspiration, trying to work out why he is different. Eventually we just accept that he is different, in some fundamental way, and while we will never understand how he does it, how he is so lacking in fear, his very existence is an inspiration.

Maybe he is just luckier than everyone else. I think of Stanley Kowalski in *Streetcar Named Desire*: 'Luck is believing you're lucky.' Maybe his ego is so large, and his self-belief so strong, he feels it is only right and reasonable to back his own judgement with everything he's got. And a bit more besides.

And of course he's had a few breaks, which we all need. But he's also smart, and highly disciplined, so you wouldn't find him arseing around like I did, when I dropped 30 on Charles Howell the Third in a golf three-ball – always a tempting market, but in truth the sporting equivalent of find-the-lady, a fairground folly.

This was slovenly punting, a 5/4 shot based on nothing more substantial than hope, an indulgence in a three-card trick which entertained me for a while on a slow afternoon, but which ultimately reversed some of the gains I had made in such a methodical fashion.

Boredom again did me down. If I ever find myself in a treatment centre for gambling, and they want me to talk about my feelings, I will speak about my feelings of abhorrence when confronted with the vacuum that is boredom.

And again it may seem like stating the bleeding obvious, but my two losers so far have come with the longest odds – 10/11 and 5/4.

The cast-iron plungers have all won.

With the cast-iron plungers, I made my selection and awaited the outcome in a state of high confidence, not some 50/50 hope.

We punters are investing enough hope already just by playing the game. Hope is a fine thing and it feels good for a little while, but in the end, as the novelist Michael Chabon put it, we are 'ruined again and again by hope'.

Charles Howell was still more likely to lose than to win, so what good was he to me? What good would he be to my man arriving in the New World with his 100 dollars?

I must keep that man in mind, because any reversal of my early gains in such a feeble-minded way is the equivalent of that man, having come so far, just frittering away his wad in a drunken game of pitch-and-toss. It is intellectually lazy and morally wrong.

Phil Mickelson, himself allegedly a gambler on the heroic scale, bails me out and restores my lead in another three-ball punt, but at the tighter price of 4/6, reflecting the strong likelihood of victory.

And then Tiger does his bit.

For me, the actual profit in real money terms is relatively slight, but it is always enlightening to observe in some detail the way Tiger does that thing that he does. If you like, you can imagine that I had thousands on him, but our purpose here is not merely to amass a fortune, but to extrapolate the inner meaning of the experience, to imagine how we might do it, if we were free.

So there was Tiger, leading the Dubai Desert Classic after two rounds, playing like God, at which point I had 70 at 2/7, because it looked like free money. And it was Tiger.

And then Tiger had one of the worst rounds of his life, leaving him four shots behind Ernie Els going in to the last day. It's no surprise to you when Charles Howell the Third lets you down, but Tiger? As his ball plopped into the water on the eighteenth, the final insult in round three, I thought of that heart-rending cry in Dostoevsky's *The Gambler*: 'what terrible jests fate sometimes plays!'

And I was working on the basis that I was now 70 down, with good reason, as Tiger could be backed at 14/1 at the tenth hole on the final day. At which point the odds started tumbling down. On the back nine, Tiger caught fire. He was playing like God again. And as he sank a downhill 40-footer for a birdie on the eighteenth, I realized that he was playing like God because he is God.

I won that 20 after all, but crucially, I don't lose 70, so we're talking about an overall swing of 90 here, which 'keeps the card going', as they say. I celebrated by taking the profit on the Ivory Coast to beat Guinea at 4/9 in the quarter-final of the Africa Cup of Nations, which is probably 'straight' enough now, at this late stage.

And later that night I congratulated myself by lying down and avoiding the Super Bowl.

Ah yes, American football has been the downfall of many a good man who couldn't resist it for no other reason than it's on the telly, round midnight, and he enjoys the novelty of betting on a live TV event in the middle of the night, weakened though he is bound to be by beer and fatigue.

At least, it used to be a novelty for punters in this part of the world to have a casual bet on the Chicago Bears to win the Super Bowl. Now the online service has made it feel like the most natural thing in the world to be watching the NFL every week with your laptop on your knee, trying to understand this awful game, picking up whatever wisdom you can glean from the barely comprehensible pundits, then entering the market, and making your move – Bet Now.

In fact you can even feel obliged on some obscure point of principle to support such worthy endeavours, as a punter and as a man.

In the mind's eye one sees Paul Merson, sitting at home with his mother one evening, betting on various markets and winning quite a large sum, and yet looking very sad all of a sudden. 'Why are you sad when you've won all that money?' his mother says.

'Because it's over,' Merse replies.

As that synergy between live TV sport and internet betting develops, with Aussie Rules or American lacrosse to be gambled on all through the night, we are reaching that point of human and technological perfection when it will never be over. Until it's over.

Famously, Merse is in recovery from his addictions, but then he could be seen punditing on Sky Sports, making predictions and generally 'calling it'. And for an addicted punter to be 'calling it' on live television is a bit like an alcoholic presenting a wine programme – obviously he can adopt a strictly professional attitude, but there must be less dangerous ways to make a living.

Still, on the good nights he would have won a lot of money, many thousands. So if Merse is reading this, despite all his difficulties he may feel that he's living better than I am. He may even regard this as the diary of a madman.

After all, the numbers involved are relatively small, yet the amount of brain-power required would suggest to some – including myself – that all things considered, I'd be better off working.

In fact when I consider the suffering I had to endure to win that 20 quid on Tiger, at times I'd be thinking that working would be a lot easier, and vastly more remunerative.

Yet when I succumb to these thoughts, I think of the billionaire Sean Quinn, who, according to legend, plays cards every Tuesday night with his buddies, happy to be betting 50 cents on a hand, with rarely more than a fiver in the pot.

Like me, Sean Quinn appreciates that a low-stakes game has most of the elements of a high-stakes game, in terms of winning and losing and the deep pleasure you feel when your judgement is vindicated. Certainly it lacks one significant element – the losing-all-your-money element.

But Sean Quinn can live with that. And the winning-loads-of-money element means nothing to him. So I guess he gets off on the primal energies of gambling, pitting his wits against an opponent, and winning. And losing. Because without the losing, the winning has no meaning.

Paradoxically, for a medium which enables an addiction to flourish wildly, for wages to be blown, for homes to be lost, and lives to be ruined, online betting also facilitates the small-stakes punter who simply wouldn't bother leaving the house to visit a real-life bookie's shop to have a fiver on a televised football match, but who would happily do it online. Just to enhance his enjoyment of the match, to back his opinion and to watch it being vindicated.

And to go completely spare if it goes the wrong way.

I would even venture to suggest that online betting has one potentially useful social function.

For the poor ould fellas whose lives have been destroyed by the smoking ban, an internet account and a decent TV service would allow them to have their few bets on the afternoon racing, and have a smoke, in their own homes – if they're still allowed to have a smoke in their own homes.

Naturally they would fiercely resist the encroachment of computer technology, because they know only too well that almost all forms of change are bad for them. And most of them would not have credit cards, on general principles and because they never buy anything anyway – on a positive note, they don't have much money to lose.

So the poor ould fellas are not exactly the most sought-after demographic by Paddy Power dot com or American Express, and yet if they could somehow get past their perfectly justified reservations, and get into the internet gambling, the poor ould fellas would discover a way to make their last days on earth vaguely bearable – unless they were so overwhelmed by its brilliance, it made them mad with rage that such a wonderful thing had been invented about five minutes before they were due to check out.

The online bookie will never query their scrawl on the betting slip, he will not make them go outside to light up, he will take their 50 cents, no problem. The online bookie aims to hoover up the 50 cents as well as the fifty grand, he doesn't care.

But I feel that the very privacy of the exercise gives the small guy a slight edge here. Guys like me and Sean Quinn, for example, would probably feel embarrassed handing a fiver across the counter of a betting office on an even-money shot, but on the laptop I don't care. It is a matter between me and God and the wizards in Alderney.

Certainly I have never backed anything at 2/7 with cash in a betting office, again because I'd be faintly ashamed. There is a mysterious tradition of secrecy and shame in the betting office, with punters hunched over their betting slips as if there's something embarrassing or even vaguely sinister going on here that must be protected from the prying eyes of others.

You rarely see men strolling contentedly around their local bookie's, happily informing anyone who cares to listen what they are backing, and why. Nor do they feel free to take the small profit, to have 20 quid on a 1/4 shot, to walk away with a paltry few euros, because somehow it doesn't seem manly.

Interestingly, the bookie never allows his machismo to get in the way of banking whatever you throw at him, however small.

He has no shame.

So the punter, liberated by the internet, can have 7 quid on a

2/7 shot, for the simple Christian pleasure of walking away from the computer with slightly more money than he had when he switched it on.

He can echo the words of another billionaire, Warren Buffett, who described his philosophy of investment thus: 'First, do not lose money.'

If it's good enough for Sean Quinn and Warren Buffett, it's good enough for the rest of us.

But of course there are times when you want a bit more out of life than that . . .   ◆

13 February 2008

♟	95 on Mickelson in two-ball @ 8/13 – **Lose**
⚫	95 on Djokovic to beat Davydenko @ 4/11 – **Lose**
⚽	85 on Man Utd to beat Man City @ 30/100 – **Lose**

. . . Even

Deposit: 100

The word 'tragedy' is freely used these days to describe all sorts of everyday misfortunes, but for once it is the right word to describe the terrible events of last weekend.

In the days leading up to Saturday, in bets too numerous to mention, I had been bobbing up and down between 200 and 270 in my account, unable to get further ahead, but still boasting a profit of roughly 100 per cent.

And then the madness started.

Phil Mickelson, one of the greatest golfers in the history of the game, had an 11 (eleven) on the fourteenth hole in the AT&T Pro-Am at Pebble Beach. I have already noted that Phil is a gambling man, so he would know that the odds on his taking an 11 (eleven), even blindfolded, with one hand tied behind his back, are incalculable.

Yet he managed it somehow, with my money riding on him. One thinks of the old golf joke: 'Question: How the heck did you have an 11 (eleven)? Answer: I missed the putt for a 10.'

And then the baleful gods dealt me another appalling blow.

Djokovic was cruising against Davydenko in the Davis Cup, two sets up and unbackable, when he became ill. Some sort of viral infection, but that doesn't matter.

One of the attractions of betting on tennis, for me and for the Russian mafia, is that you have no draws. It's either win or lose, except on those rare occasions when a player retires ill or injured, thus forfeiting the match, and, more importantly, all the bets placed on him. On Blue Square, at least.

This was one such rare occasion. And I didn't see the illness happening, because when I checked out the match on Sky, it had ended. I assumed it had ended in victory for Djokovic, because at two sets down, when I checked it about twenty minutes later, Davydenko simply wouldn't have had the time to win the next three sets. All day, in fact, I assumed that this was money in the bank, which consoled me somewhat as I watched Man Utd losing at home to Man City, who were 12/1 at the start. This was hardly a bet at all, it was what we call 'buying money'.

Instead it bought me tragedy, compounded by the eventual discovery that Djokovic had indeed lost. He had been taken to hospital, but that doesn't matter.

I am back where I started, left with no option but to replenish my funds by making another successful deposit of 100. I guess the equivalent for my man just arrived in America is to break into some emergency fund that he keeps in his shoe.

Yet it is strangely fascinating to be laid low with such brutality. Being rigorously honest, I really can't blame myself for such a triple whammy, such an absurd sequence of events happening within twenty-four hours.

Indeed it suggests that the baleful gods had come to regard me as a genuine threat, that they feared I was on an upward spiral which would eventually lead to a profit of thousands. And they don't like upward spirals. The baleful gods like downward spirals.

Yet there is much food for thought here. For a while there, when I was ahead, I was half-regretting and even three-quarters regretting that I hadn't started with 1,000. Or even 10,000. So I dodged the bullet there.

And I genuinely feel I did nothing wrong. I feel that I called it right, and those guys just let me down.

Dark forces, I feel, are messing with me.

And it illustrates what the betting man is up against, how even his most sensible investments can be undone.

I believe that at a time like this, a punter of the stature of Barney Curley just stops betting for a while and takes himself off to America or somewhere, until he feels the tide has turned again. When he senses that he has lost his touch, and the baleful gods are doing him down, he doesn't fight it.

So I will resume the diary when I feel that the force is with me again. This is a long campaign after all – it lasts until September.

In the aftermath of this attack, I need some perspective. In fact I think I need to go back about thirty-five years to figure out how I got to this place.

A Bit of Previous
THREE-STAR CAST-IRON PLUNGERS

I TAKE THIS 'biographical reminiscence' device from Flann O'Brien's *At Swim-Two-Birds*, in which O'Brien's main character digresses into his personal history, as he receives racing tips through the post from one Verney Wright, a 'Turf Correspondent' with an address at Wyvern Cottage, Newmarket, Suffolk.

I was doing something similar at the age of sixteen, at least partly influenced by my reading of *At Swim-Two-Birds*, which reflects the ancient nature of our quest. Scott Eagle was the man who supplied me with his version of Verney Wright's 'three-star cast-iron plungers'.

I had been so impressed by Scott Eagle's advertisement in some racing paper, I sent off my postal order for £1.50 or whatever to receive a weekly bulletin containing the names of horses that were going to win on the Saturday.

Like the protagonist in *At Swim-Two-Birds*, I was an educated young man of reasonable intelligence, and yet I was somehow in thrall to the wisdom of men like Scott Eagle.

I hadn't even considered the logistics involved in Scott Eagle's posting his cast-iron plungers to me from London, supposedly to arrive in the seaside village of Blackrock outside Dundalk in the Republic of Ireland, before the Saturday. Even though my aunt, with whom I spent all my summer holidays in Blackrock, was also the postmistress, some of those cast-iron plungers just didn't get through. And when they eventually arrived the following week I would mostly be glad that they hadn't got through.

But there were no hard feelings, and for years afterwards I kept receiving these mysterious missives from various addresses in England advising me that there was money to be made. That it was out there, just waiting to be picked up by any man with the stomach for the task, and the good fortune to be receiving the names of racing certainties every week through the post.

Scott Eagle was no more, his mantle had apparently been taken over by men with different false names, who were equally 'in the know'. I would study these amazing offers with the contempt they deserved, throwing them away after about three seconds.

Well, three minutes.

OK, I probably still have a few stashed away somewhere.

18 February 2008

- 100 on Murray to beat Ancic @ 1/2 – **Win**
- 50 on Mickelson in three-ball @ 4/5 – **Win**

. . . −10

Back on the horse again.

But then like any punter I am almost endlessly resilient. I

may take the most heart-breaking blows. I may be genuinely out of the game for days, even weeks, my morale shattered by what I have lost, and how I have lost it. I may be consumed with feelings of guilt and shame and impotent rage.

But that too will pass. Because I just can't stop trying for another winner. I want that heightened reality, I want to live in that moment again. I want to have a dog in the fight.

It is one of the most ancient challenges posed to the punter, this business of starting over and over again, trying to make it different this time. Something about the 'clean slate' (in large quotation marks) seems to raise your performance. You fool yourself into thinking that this is all very measured and controlled. That you won't be fooled again.

And then you have a winner, and maybe another winner, and then somehow you start to lose your way. Of course you don't think you're going to lose your way. You never have a bet thinking you're going to lose. But you find yourself betting impulsively on something you haven't properly assessed, thinking that your impulses are often as good as your well-reasoned judgements.

And you might be right about that, sometimes, but perhaps the main mistake you make is being there at all. Because somehow you will always find that way to go backwards.

It's a bit of a catch-22: you are right to think that a certain football team will win the game, and your sound judgement is to be applauded. But by dint of your forming that opinion, and backing it, automatically it follows that the team cannot now win the game.

Even when you are feeling most in control of the situation, wisely marshalling your resources, you are labouring under a fundamental misapprehension – you may be feeling like

General Dwight D. Eisenhower, calmly monitoring the situation in the war room, successfully plotting the Normandy landings. But in fact your situation is more akin to that of the boys trying to stay alive as they scramble out of the boats in the first half-hour of *Saving Private Ryan*.

You do not know the time or the hour.

And now with the internet option, it becomes almost humanly impossible to dodge the proverbial bullets.

You might be well ahead, with hundreds in your account, and you tune in to the last five minutes of a friendly international, say, England v Belarus. You have no intention of having a bet. And yet you can feel the old urge, stirring deep within you.

And you see that England are leading 1–0 at home against Belarus. In days of yore, using the conventional betting methods, even if you felt that old urge, you would come to no harm. Even if the bookie's office opened late, you just wouldn't bother getting yourself down there for a bet on the last ten minutes of a nothing game. But now you log on to your internet betting provider and you see that England are 1/10 'in-running'. It looks to you like free money.

Impulsively, you fancy that you'll take the quick profit – your first thought is usually the best, right?

It takes you about four seconds to have 400 on England to win 40, the deed is done, and now you can relax while you watch the rest of the game, waiting to collect that 40 quid, building up your ammunition, working the system to your advantage for a change.

Except it doesn't quite work like that. With the money down, the dying minutes of this dreary old match suddenly become a thing of terrible intensity for you. And now you are seeing danger everywhere, because it appears that you are the only person alive who gives a damn about the result, the only person for whom there is something at stake.

Two minutes into added time, Belarus get an equalizer. Nobody cares, it's only a friendly, but you are destroyed.

Happens all the time.

Which is not to say that a bet you have been carefully considering for six months is inherently better or more likely to succeed. You just feel like less of a chump when it gets away from you.

But here I am, back on the horse again, anyway.

I have endless belief in Andy Murray, enough to stake my entire wad on him. And I figured that Big Swinging Mickelson mightn't have another 11 for some time. But today I am greatly exercised by events off the park, as it were.

Statto has been declared bankrupt. Angus Loughran aka Statto, tipster for the BBC and the *Telegraph*, officially a 'sports consultant', and a first-rate fellow, is unable to pay his creditors and has been declared insolvent. The bankruptcy order involved council tax arrears.

A Bit of Previous
THE WHISKEY AND THE BEER AND THE CIGAR SMOKE AND THE HORSE SHIT

THE FIRST SERIOUS ambition I had in life was to be a bookie. For a punter to feel that he would like to be the guy on the other side of the deal didn't strike me at the time as a sign of my weakness. I was just vastly impressed in a childlike way by the obvious attractions of being a bookie, which I would note on my big days out at the races.

Essentially it seemed that these were men who arrived at the races in very big cars, and who stood at the rails with large satchels stuffed with money exuding an air of invincibility.

Why would you want to be anything else?

My father Frank, or the father of my best friend Paul O'Neill, who was also called Frank, would take us to the races. I think the first time must have been Laytown, where they have been racing on the strand since 1868. I was perhaps ten years old, so it was probably my Frank who took me there. But no doubt the other Frank, an Armagh lawyer and a serious punter who went racing with a bunch of his Northern buddies, was there or thereabouts.

I backed a winner that day, at least my father backed it for me on the Tote, or so he said. He was a relaxed backer who didn't need the buzz of having a bet on every race, and he probably thought that I too would have the gift of calmness.

I think the horse he backed for me was called Bay Tree. I can't recall how much I won, but it was probably about two quid. I know that the feeling was sensational, and maybe this is what keeps men going until they reach the gates of hell. Like heroin, the winners feel so good you just keep trying to recapture that feeling even when it's destroying you.

Maybe it's the feeling of that first winner that you keep trying to replicate. Like the alcoholic with his first drink, it's like discovering a form of magic that turns the world into a better place for you.

A therapist might tell me that punting is my way of connecting with my father, and the happiest days of our lives. For about ten years after that first epiphany at Laytown, during the summer months, with one Frank or the other, we went to most of the tracks in the east of Ireland.

I loved them all unconditionally, especially Phoenix Park ('the Park'), which has since been destroyed, a calamity for Dublin and for mankind. I collected racecards which I would 'read' again and again on the long nights after Samhain (Hallowe'en) to relive those days at Dundalk and Fairyhouse and the Curragh and Navan and Naas and the Park.

I was perhaps one of the youngest men in Ireland to seriously consider sending off for the Form Book. And I would make a written note of the daily racing results which were read out on RTE Radio, storing up information, or 'ammunition', until it was time to go racing again.

It was overwhelming stuff for me, the colour, the adrenalin, the intrigue. I can still smell those race meetings, the whiskey and the beer and the cigar smoke and the horse shit.

Ah, the whiskey and the smoke and the horse shit, and the excitement of being dispatched with Paul by the adults to listen in to the conversations of known 'players', and reporting back, like spies.

The therapist might even tell me that this was a rite of passage, this eavesdropping on the talk of owners and trainers and occasionally even Barney Curley himself, entering the dark world of men by stealth.

Curley in particular, in his hat and his trench coat, had become an iconic figure since the Yellow Sam coup, a coup which broke no law, and which went off at Bellewstown in the summer of 1975 in a way which illustrates how far we have come, and how we are somehow still the same.

The Yellow Sam coup would have been utterly inconceivable today. It was not just pre-internet, it seems almost medieval, as it depended entirely for its success on the wonderfully simple premise that there was only one public phone at Bellewstown racecourse. So for the betting offices to contact the on-course bookies to tell them about the enormous moneys being punted on Yellow Sam, and to slash the starting price accordingly, they would have to make a call to this phone. Which was unfortunately occupied for about half an hour, or enough time for Yellow Sam to win his race, with no money on him at the track, ensuring a starting price of 20/1 and a profit of about 300 grand from all those bets in the offices.

Today betting men are still incessantly trying to find ways to catch the enemy sleeping, in a world in which everybody is on the record, on camera, on tape, or on the computer, in which everything that can possibly be known is known and can easily be proved. And still men dream of another Yellow Sam, the coup which has assumed the same exalted place in the consciousness of punters as the Cuban revolution has in the hearts of the oppressed – it is a holy thing.

For a punter such as my unworthy self to have stood beside Curley when he was at his most charismatic, trying to listen in to his conversations, is a bit like the lifelong socialist who can truthfully claim that he once sat on a bar stool in Bolivia next to Che Guevara and found him very down-to-earth.

Curley, of course, doesn't drink. And neither do I – at least, not since Christmas 1995.

At least, not today.

So we never picked up much in the way of loose talk from Curley, but there were always other personalities to be stalked, and we were indefatigable.

On a stand-out day at the Park, Paul and I were sent by his Frank to follow Mrs Magnier, the wife of the trainer Clem Magnier, who was having a bet of 50p on the Tote. Essentially, we just had to ascertain whether she was backing her own horse, which would suggest that the stable was confident in the outcome. We listened hard as we stood behind her in the queue, and as she spoke the number of the horse she wanted to back, we were able to establish that indeed she was backing her own horse, called Molly Pitcher as I recall, and moreover I recall that Molly Pitcher won at 13/2.

Again the therapist would suggest that this initiation into the ways of the adult world had a profound impression on me. That for the rest of my life I have been trying to recapture the joy of making a winning contribution on that day.

Like Mrs Magnier, Paul and I were still betting on the Tote, but soon we were to reach the next stage in our journey to punting maturity, leaving the queue at the Tote to the women and children, to bet like men with the bookies.

Indeed one of the deepest attractions of being a bookie was that you got to go to race meetings all the time. And even after I realized that people like me just didn't have whatever it takes to be a bookie, it remained my childhood ambition to get a job, any job, which provided me with a car in which I could take myself to race meetings under my own steam, at which point my happiness would be complete. This was the dream: any time you like you get into your car, you point it in the direction of a race meeting and you go there. Result? Happiness.

And the primary ambition to be a bookie wasn't just a pipedream. I had figured that the village of Blackrock needed a betting office, because otherwise you had to get the bus into Dundalk, three miles away.

As a youth I correctly foresaw the growth of Blackrock from a seaside village into the wealthy extension of Dundalk that it is today, though I didn't quite foresee the internet, which would make a betting office in Blackrock less of an absolute necessity. I had even selected my premises, a little butcher's shop that sold fancy German sausages near the top of the village. Again I had correctly predicted that the fancy German sausages shop wouldn't be there long.

I had ascertained that you needed a 'bond', and not much else, to become a bookie. Not much else, that is, except a head for figures, which I didn't have – I just hoped I'd get away with that one.

All these plans were buzzing in my head at a time when my elders assumed I was going to be a lawyer or somesuch. And in theory, anyway, I wouldn't have minded becoming a lawyer, because Paul O'Neill's father was a lawyer and he went to loads of race meetings with other lawyers; in fact their lives seemed to comprise about ninety-five parts racing to five parts lawyering, and as such it was a beautiful life. They needed it too, to escape from the Troubles, which in the mid-1970s were at their most grotesque.

There was a bunch of them who came down to the racetracks of the Republic as often as was humanly possible, to get away from the National Question, and to seek solace in more uplifting aspects of the human spirit, such as trying to figure out who was 'trying' and who wasn't.

These men are all dead now; spookily, they all died within a relatively short period. We formed the strong impression that they had discovered some sort of punting heaven where everyone is trying all the time.

Sadly my own ambitions were changing with the acceptance that I just didn't have that bookie-gene. But the first article I wrote for publication was a piece for the school magazine about going to race meetings.

My younger brother Damien never had my ambition, or my obsession with the turf. He tells me now he was amused to find that school books of mine which were handed down to him used to have betting slips tucked away inside them – losing slips, of course.

He went off to London a few years later and did a bit of teaching for a while. Then he became a bookie.

A MOMENT OF SOBER REFLECTION
ANYONE FOR A BIT OF CLAY COURT ACTION FROM ROMANIA?

They say that the rehab clinics are filling up with addicted gamblers, most of them men, most of them men of high intelligence. Men who are so intelligent, it seems, they are prepared to back their brain power to the hilt. Men who, for all their intelligence, do not understand that the same addiction centres have always been full of men of high intelligence who just couldn't stop drinking. Because somehow these things are not just about intelligence; in fact your intelligence can keep your addiction going at full pelt, because it feeds your ego.

In your egotistical way, you keep thinking you're a smart guy who wouldn't be doing something silly like becoming an alcoholic or a compulsive gambler. For the gambler, intelligence will only take you so far in a world in which even the grand old game of tennis has attracted the attention of the Russian mafia, and almost every day brings some new report about 'unusual betting patterns'.

The Malta Open snooker tournament was mentioned in the context of allegations of our old friend 'unusual betting patterns'. And, lest we forget, allegedly there were 'unusual betting patterns' at the Africa Cup of Nations which the world has decided simply to forget.

In Antwerp, a couple of German guys and the inevitable Russian were thrown out of a women's tennis tournament for allegedly using their battery-powered laptops to bet on points being scored a split-second before the points registered on the internet – just another bunch of guys looking for an edge.

Here they were attempting to take advantage of the 'in-running' market, whereby the prices change constantly as the event takes shape, and if in that split second you can press the button which says 'Bet Now' . . .

Mind you, I have to question those guys who just happened to be implementing their cunning plan at a women's tennis tournament in Belgium, which presumably had about twelve spectators at it, thus making them a tad conspicuous with their laptops.

The tournament was shown live on Eurosport, which means that no one would have to actually go there unless it was absolutely necessary. But then punters all over Europe would be watching it for betting purposes. It seems clear that most tennis on TV, or anywhere else for that matter, is for betting purposes.

And if it's not on the telly, there's an ATP website on which you can 'watch' every point racking up on a scoreboard, in every game of ATP tennis being played, anywhere in the world, as it happens. It's a beautiful thing, this website scoreboard, and there are multitudes who now 'watch' tennis matches in this way, forming the most pungent opinions on what they are 'watching', without actually seeing a ball being struck.

Anyone for a bit of clay court action from Romania this afternoon?

And at this time of year, our thoughts are also with all those men who went down on the night of the Super Bowl. Yes, we think of them now, imagining the past as we constantly try to imagine the future.

In these dark visions we see them unable to take themselves away from the American football, which, it is worth restating, is the downfall of many a good man.

In the mind's eye we can see these men, deep in the hole, having one last massive punt on the New England Patriots, who are a 'lock', as the Americans put it, to win the Super Bowl. One last big job that will bail them out if they win, and sink them once and for all if they lose. Except, of course, they're not going to lose because the Patriots are a 'lock'.

Perhaps they remembered their prayers and whispered a few Hail Marys, to help the Patriots close the deal, the Patriots who seemed so certain of victory, against the Giants. As certain as . . . Oh, as certain as Man Utd were certain to beat Man City at home last week.

And in our fearful imaginings, we see them staying up half the night, with the Patriots under pressure from the Giants all the way, but staying ahead until the last throw of the ball game. Touchdown for the Giants. Game over.

And the game is in its dying moments too for Mr Graham Calvert, a promising greyhound trainer who is suing William Hill because, terrified by his mounting losses, he alleges that he asked Hill's not to take any more of his bets, a system known as 'self-exclusion'. He claimed that they continued taking his bets until he was down roughly £2 million. William Hill is claiming otherwise and is an unbackable favourite to win.

This man had £347,000 on America to win the Ryder Cup at the K Club.

> Myself, I had 80 euros on the Americans @ 5/4, and when they lost I was gutted. Absolutely facking gutted.

25 February 2008

- 40 on Chela to beat Ventura @ 4/7 – **Win**
- 30 on Kaymer to beat Weekley @ 4/5 – **Lose**
- 40 on Toms to beat Johnson @ 5/6 – **Win**
- 30 on Tosic to beat Duque Marino @ 5/6 – **Lose**
- 70 on Horna to beat Gonzalez @ 4/11 – **Win**
- 100 on Mickelson to beat Perez @ 4/11 – **Win**
- 40 on Harrington to beat Cink @ 4/7 – **Lose**
- 40 on Westwood to beat Leonard @ 8/11 – **Lose**
- 20 on Calleri to beat Horna @ 4/7 – **Win**
- 30 on Karlovic to beat Zverev @ 4/11 – **Win**
- 40 on Stenson to beat Byrd @ 8/13 – **Win**
- 20 on Karlovic to beat Llodra @ 4/7 – **Lose**
- 150 on Woods to win World Matchplay @ 6/5 – **Win**

. . . +180

It is the Monday morning after Tiger beat my nemesis Stewart Cink by 8 & 7 in the final of the Accenture World Matchplay, and I am showing the sort of percentage profit that Warren Buffett himself might regard as fanciful. Certainly it's a hell of a lot more than you'll be getting at the Bradford & Bingley. Maybe there's hope for this quest.

It is the fruit of a tough week campaigning in the South American tennis markets and the North American golf markets, areas in which I am not an acknowledged world expert, but in which my instincts are evidently quite sound.

After all, the record shows I had roughly twice as many winners as losers. But in this notoriously harsh climate for investors, that was still not enough to break even. At these prices, any loser will suck the life out of you. And I confess that I was losing heart when Harrington lost to Cink, and Westwood lost to Leonard at the Accenture Matchplay, pushing me back down the hill again, like Sisyphus.

Actually I am now convinced that the myth of Sisyphus was inspired by the sufferings of punters in ancient Greece. Yes, after a particularly unfortunate run of results at the Games, it would be natural to conceive of that image of the man pushing the rock up the hill again and again and again. After all, the enduring power of Greek mythology is based on the notion that the human condition is the same today as it was in ancient times, that the Greeks had just the same hopes and fears back then as we have today. And therefore they had the same, yes, Sisyphean struggles trying to get ahead, and to stay ahead.

But the one thing they didn't have back then that we have today is a thing called Tiger Woods.

Like I say, I was losing heart. I was despondent. I was thinking that this diary was showing me in the coldest terms the utter futility of this punting life in a way that had never been so clear to me before, all these cruel setbacks calling to mind Orwell's image of the boot stamping on the human face, for ever.

And then, almost in despair, when I was seriously wondering if I was reaching the end of my journey, I spotted an opportunity to put one of my most deeply held beliefs into practice.

I saw that after the first round of the Accenture World Matchplay, Tiger Woods was 6/5. With four rounds still to be played, I plunged. I had the biggest bet of this campaign so far, at the biggest odds. Because as I always say, picking winners is not necessarily the problem. We can pick winners all day long. What we can't do is pick our moment so that we derive the maximum possible return from our winners.

So I picked my moment. And at a time like this, you need a Tiger out there doing it for you, a Tiger who is the punting equivalent of a blue-chip investment. Because even if you're putting your proverbial house on him, or perhaps £347,000, he transmits a sense of security to you that you just don't get from your top-ranking South American tennis player.

Then again, maybe Graham Calvert felt that deep, deep sense of security radiating from Tiger just before the Ryder Cup at the K Club . . . but I digress.

There will be other days for remembering our fallen comrades. Today, we'll try to absorb the lessons of our success. And one of the more painful lessons is that in punting, as in life, less is more.

Essentially, we should be having fewer bets. We place ourselves at the mercy of the baleful gods too many times. And the online phenomenon has done much to encourage such profligacy.

They're offering you odds on every damn thing, the most notable recent example on Blue Square being a market on Danish women's handball. Now, the punter who wants to have a bit of fun will have his fiver on the Danish women's handball and let the devil take the hindmost.

But like the American football, this 'fun' can cost lives.

For a long time now, betting corporations have been pushing this 'fun' shit, with spokesmen for Paddy Power in particular appearing frequently in the media to price up all sorts of events 'just for a bit of fun', and to offer 'hilarious' odds like, say, 200/1 on Jack Charlton to become the next President of Ireland.

In fact this has nothing at all to do with fun, but with a long-term corporate strategy to change the image of gambling from a sordid activity akin to back-street abortion, indulged in by broken men and bad women, into some sort of family entertainment. And it has been a tremendously successful strategy. Even the recent election of a Catholic bishop was 'priced up' by bookies in Northern Ireland, who then received a load of free publicity when they reported that 'insider' betting, presumably by Catholic priests, had cost the bookies about seven grand in bets placed at prices ranging from 7/1 down to 5/4.

'This is the first time we have had to pay out in the relatively small market of church appointments,' the PR lady said. Apparently they had broken even on the election of Pope Benedict.

We can only stand in admiration of the PR lady speaking about the 'relatively small market of church appointments', as if it were a mundane and logical development in the gaming industry. There was a time when this would have sounded as outlandish as the old stereotype of the two flies crawling up a wall; now it is normal to be giving odds on two bishops crawling up the ecclesiastical ladder.

The hit they took on the bishop in Northern Ireland represented a saving of many thousands when you consider all the free advertising supplied by their media stooges in the name of fun.

Put it like this: if bookies wanted you to bet less frequently, you would click open your online service and you'd see two or three markets for the month, instead of roughly 2,000 for the day. You may find it more 'fun' to peruse this vast array of sporting chances, but you can be sure that your enemies who are providing you with all this fun are not themselves doing it for fun.

In fact there is no greater certainty than that.

So on a slow day like today, the bookies, in association with their good friends in television, are heavily promoting Milton

Keynes Dons v Swansea City, which is live on Sky Sports. In fact most Monday nights, live on Sky or Setanta, there's some low-down football match, sometimes as low as a 'non-league' match, which is sponsored by the good people at Blue Square.

Indeed.

And terrifying amounts are wagered on these lowdown affairs, by men who just can't stop themselves, men who couldn't get through a Monday without the prospect of a Monday-night bet on something – anything – that is being shown on the telly.

Otherwise this Monday offers such fine fare as a tennis match between Stephanie Cohen-Aloro and Michelle Lacharde Brito, for Christ's sake, which is happening somewhere in the world at 4 p.m., and which can no doubt be 'watched' on the ATP website. Or racing on the all-weather at Wolverhampton.

We've all been there, and hell, many of us will be there tonight. Because we are weak. Because we just want to have fun.

But the example of the Tiger tells us that we must, if at all possible, direct our attention away from Milton Keynes Dons, away from doubles, trebles and accumulators, from Trixies, Trifectas, Yankees, Fourfolds, Penfolds, Patents, Heinzes, Superheinzes, Lucky Fifteens, and something called a Goliath, and towards the blue-chip investments, towards performers of the highest quality, who will carry our money on the nose, as if it was their own.

Not that you can bet on Tiger every day. But if you can get anything better than Evens on Tiger, to win anything, at any time, you should go out and back him. In fact you should go out and back him all day.

And when you come home you should sit down and think about it for a while.

And then you should go out and back him again.

A Bit of Previous
THE SACKING OF HACKETT'S

IT MAY HAVE occurred to the reader that of all the bets so far, none has involved a horse, a greyhound, or indeed any animal other than the human.

As a boy racing enthusiast, I could scarcely conceive of any form of betting other than betting on horses, and the occasional dog, partly because there was little else available.

Now, after thinking deeply on this for many years, I have come to the sad but irreversible decision that there is something inherently foolish about betting on horses. And betting on dogs is not just inherently foolish, it is almost immoral.

I guess the horses just wore me down over the years, to the extent that these days I would have the odd punt on the Classics or at Cheltenham, a bit like the mythical housewife but without the bit of luck with which the baleful gods favour the mythical housewife. I know too much for that.

And yet, by comparison with where I used to be as a boy racer, I know too little. I followed the horses so avidly back then, I was giving myself at least half a chance. And I don't think I could ever get back to that feverish dedication you need at the top level.

I'm not good enough for the horses any more, and coincidentally, the horses are not good enough for me. Obviously the good races are all still there, with most of the horses trying to some extent. But overwhelmingly the daily stuff of the track is what you see at Wolverhampton and Southwell, the sort of fare that Barney Curley was thinking about when he described the bookie's ideal day as one in which he 'recycles all the dole money and takes his rake-off'.

All that bad, bad racing full of bad, bad horses on which no man should be expected to place his money. Yet place it he does, mainly because he can find nothing else to bet on at that time of the day, and he needs something to bet on, he needs it desperately. And after all, a race full of bad horses can still provide an exciting finish, even if they're running very slowly.

Increasingly, though, even the traditionalists are seeking other outlets. In conjunction with the general move from the offices to the internet, roughly 50 per cent of all betting is on sports other than racing, where once racing used to be roughly 95 per cent. The punter is investing in sports that he might be watching anyway, if he hadn't money on it. He is betting on football and golf to enhance his TV experience, whereas he would rarely bet on a race for the extra pleasure it might afford – usually, the bet is the only pleasure it affords him, particularly if the race is at Musselburgh on a Monday.

He is even investing in the Virtual Racing, a form of pretend racing which, for all that, seems at least as satisfying as anything going down at Towcester or Lingfield. As one bookmaker told me, 'When the Virtual Racing first came in, everyone stood there and laughed. They thought it was complete bollocks, looking at pretend horses running their race, with a fake commentary. Then after a while you'd see the hands going into the pockets, and maybe a tenner coming out, just for pig-iron. Then you'd see the hands going into the pockets again . . .'

And as the craving for action intensifies, I can see an increasing demand for betting on Virtual Football, Virtual Snooker, Virtual-Anything-That-Moves, because humans are just not able to keep the punters supplied with enough actual sport to satisfy their needs.

My God, on certain days – Christmas for example – there is almost nothing to bet on until the darts starts up again at the Ally Pally, an ingenious invention that has eased the punter's Yuletide pain. Now he can forget about the brouhaha surrounding Jesus' birthday and get all his Christmas money back on Raymond van Barneveld. After a lifetime of seasonal suffering he is liberated by the smooth release of a Dutchman's arrow.

There will be Virtual Darts too, when the real stuff ends as it always does and punters realize the beauty of eliminating all that human weakness. They are even letting women play darts on TV these days, something that would never be allowed to happen in the Virtual world.

And no doubt I'll succumb to some of these pleasures at least, though I have honestly never had a bet on a Virtual Race, perhaps as a mark of respect to the better class of racing that once captivated me, and in deference to what I have achieved in the game.

I am, after all, the man who once spent the afternoon betting in Hackett's of Dun Laoghaire, and who had to collect his winnings at Hackett's of Sallynoggin, because they didn't have enough cash to pay me at the end of the day at the Dun Laoghaire branch.

The fact that I achieved this while half-drunk makes it all the more remarkable. It had started as an afternoon of drinking, which just developed into an afternoon of drinking and betting, organically, as it were.

As the winners kept coming, the drink should have screwed me in the end, by persuading me to lose it all in one heroic punt, but somehow, astoundingly, that never happened. And when I went to the pay-out window for the sixth or seventh time, the girl had to apologize to me on behalf of the Hackett organization, whose Dun Laoghaire branch I had just cleaned out, after accumulated winnings of roughly £300 – and, in 1989, £300 was £300.

This day of dazzling achievement was matched only by the day at the Park when I 'went through the card'. I say I 'went through the card', even though the card had seven races, and I didn't actually back the winner of the first. But when you back six winners in a row, you can say you went through the card, in fact you can say anything you like, because you have done something so rare, and so wondrous.

I did it sober too, my mind concentrated perhaps by the fact that I had an unsteady income as a journalist, and I now had a baby daughter to support. But sobriety aside, the six-in-a-row resembled the sacking of Hackett's in its lack of premeditation.

For example, in retrospect I would have won the Jackpot, but of course I wasn't betting in retrospect, I was just having tenners and twenties on individual races, assuming with each bet that I simply couldn't have another winner, statistically, morally or any other way. And still the buggers kept winning, at big fat prices like 5/2, 7/2, 11/2, certainly nothing less than 2/1.

We got a taxi home that day – keep the change, baby! – and yet, as I got that taxi from the Park all the way to Dun Laoghaire, high on the improbability of it all, again with about £300 in raw bookies' cash, I had mixed feelings.

I knew that I had achieved some sort of a punting miracle with my six-in-a-row, and a few hundred quid of the bookies' money is always useful for a young man with a baby daughter. Yet I also knew that if the proverbial Barney Curley had achieved the same miracle, he would also have achieved winnings which were greatly in excess of a few hundred quid.

So I felt a bit like the country'n'Irish singer Brian Coll, a retired gambler (who I recently discovered was once in a showband managed by the same Barney Curley), who recalled in a TV documentary, presented by the excellent Shay Healy, how he greatly fancied Little Owl to win the Cheltenham Gold Cup, because he had seen a small boy playing with a little owl, and took this as an omen.

Coll had been on a losing streak, but so strong was the omen, he called his bookie and had £400 on Little Owl at 9/1. And then, assailed by doubts, he lost his bottle. He called back and changed the stake to £100.

So when Little Owl duly won the Gold Cup, Brian Coll won £900. And still he was not happy. He was ruing what he would have won if he'd backed his original inspiration to the hilt. Because, like me, he knew that such inspiration does not come easily, and in fact it might never come again.

He was unhappy when he was losing, and now he was unhappy even when he was winning.

'When I was wrong I was wrong, and even when I was right I was wrong,' Coll reflected. And his response was to give up gambling for good.

I, rightly or wrongly, have kept the faith.

3 March 2008

- ⚽ 30 on Man City to beat Everton 'Draw No Bet' – **Lose**
- ♏ 40 on India to beat Sri Lanka @ 4/6 – **Win**
- ⚽ 40 on Barcelona to beat Atletico Madrid @ 5/6 – **Lose**
- ⚽ 30 on Everton to beat Portsmouth @ 10/11 – **Win**
- ⛳ 50 on Ernie Els to win Honda Classic @ Evens – **Win**
- ⛳ 150 on Lorena Ochoa to win HSBC Champions tournament @ 11/10 – **Win**
- ⚫ 100 lost on tennis matches in highly suspicious circumstances

. . . +310

In the Business Report on *Morning Ireland* on RTE Radio, they were talking about 'the rise and rise of online gambling', and a great year all round for Paddy Power.

They weren't talking about me, though I'm now reporting a percentage profit which in the corporate sector would entitle me to a massive, massive bonus – and now that I think of it I'd be getting a massive, massive bonus anyway, regardless of my performance, just for being in the corporate sector.

On the face of it, the above figures and that impressive bottom line represent another triumphant surge, though a quick calculation will tell the reader that the figures are in-complete for reasons that I'll explain in a moment.

What is beyond question is that I have again followed one of my core beliefs, and been lavishly rewarded for this by the merciful gods. For some time now I have been following the career of the Mexican golfer Lorena Ochoa with interest. I had never heard of her until I opened my internet account and saw that they were offering prices on women's golf. They don't talk much about women's golf on the floor of your local betting shop, but on Blue Square we are free to indulge our basest instincts. We have become aficionados.

Confusingly, about twenty of the world's leading players are from Korea, and are called Kim – an edge there, for the bookies. But Ochoa stands alone, the leading female player in the world by some distance for at least a year. And in that time I have probably taken more profit on Ochoa than on any other living thing. You could say she is the female Tiger – or the Tigress, as my sportswriting colleagues might dub her. And I feel that my deep understanding of her dominance has given me an 'edge' in the little-known female golf markets, which I have exploited online with considerable prowess.

The punter is always looking for an 'edge', real or imaginary. There are men who claim a unique expertise on Davis Cup tennis matches, for example, who will stake large sums on these obscure and largely meaningless events, feeling that the bookies are not paying enough attention, and are pricing them up too generously, a rare oversight for which the punter must exact maximum retribution.

So when I saw that Ochoa was leading by a shot after the first round of the HSBC Champions tournament, and was 11/10 to win outright, I made my move. Taking my own advice that you should reserve your biggest stakes for what might be called the blue-chip investments, the Tigers and indeed the Tigresses, I matched the 150 I had invested in Tiger, at odds slightly better than Evens. And when I checked the tournament website the next morning, Ochoa had extended her lead to seven shots. Which is the golf equivalent of being 3–0 up at half time, with the opposition down to ten men. And she was now 1/20 on Blue Square.

Indeed.

While I slept, Ochoa had been working for me in Singapore – in brisk overnight trading I had made significant gains. And while I would never entirely rule out some unimaginable catastrophe doing me down, I was able to savour the moment. I had made my investment in a way that was verging on the scientific. I had felt a rush of confidence when I saw that Ochoa was leading and still backable, a physical sensation that was essentially different from the usual mixture of emotions you feel when you're contemplating a punt, the usual impulses of confidence and doubt and hope and caution and whatever you feel when you discover at the last moment that the price has shortened.

So these rare rushes of pure confidence are to be noted, and acted upon – with the proviso that the baleful gods are always there or thereabouts, and may be seizing their moment too.

But what else have we to guide us through this eternal night? How can we fail to respond to our own best instincts here?

Clearly there are matters of brain chemistry involved in all aspects of punting. No matter how well we rationalize it, no matter how many times we add it all up and say 'never again', the gambling juices continue to spring from their primal sources, flooding the brain regardless. In fact the more we need them to stop, the more copiously they flow, and the more irreparable the damage. So we must somehow recognize the vastly complex signals which our brain is sending us, both in assessing our state of addiction and in our search for winners.

It is all too much.

Is our first instinct always the best? Or are we best served by a less gung-ho approach? And how are we supposed to pick a winner when our brain chemistry is further altered by the effects of alcohol?

Generally speaking, the proximity of so many betting offices to pubs, and the evident success of those offices, is probably no coincidence. Yet when I cleaned out Hackett's of Dun Laoghaire I was half-drunk . . . totally drunk by close of business, if truth be told.

I could muse much on these intriguing physiological and psychiatric issues, but I should confirm that after three rounds in Singapore Ochoa was leading by eight shots. And she eventually won by a ridiculous eleven shots.

It was the perfect bet, virtually tension-free. But perhaps the real achievement of these last few days has been the consolidation of those gains, in the most hostile conditions.

I kept all but about 30 euros of the Ochoa winnings, largely through the wise punting I have detailed above, but also in spite of a number of bizarre reversals on the tennis courts that I have not listed for reasons that will become obvious.

I haven't listed them because I just don't believe some of those tennis results.

Top players such as Andy Murray have spoken of this, with Murray pointing out that the struggling tennis pro is making so little money for getting knocked out in the first round of a tournament he is open to temptation.

Again, there is this inherent beauty in tennis for the gambler – there are no draws. And for the gambler who likes to know the outcome in advance, there's the added attraction that it's so easy to fix a match – you knock a few balls wide at the right time and the job is done, and no one can call you on it. Or you just retire injured, ideally having won the first set, at which point various sums are mysteriously placed on the other guy, whose odds have lengthened because he is so far behind – it's our old friend 'unusual betting patterns'.

And if there's one thing worse than the proverbial afternoon tennis match live on Eurosport from Romania, it's a bent after-noon tennis match live on Eurosport from Romania.

Yet even in these hazardous conditions, I was still mostly ahead on the tennis betting. I had an assured touch until recently, when I found myself for the first time completely bamboozled by various results that were going down.

And my defeats in recent days might have devoured the Ochoa winnings but for an exceptionally strong performance in other markets. I refer especially to that 50 on Ernie Els at Evens to win the Honda Classic, a bet which merits elucida-tion, because it was as haphazard as the Ochoa bet was deeply felt.

My friend the top sportswriter Dion Fanning phoned me because the Honda Classic was on Setanta, and he fancied a bet. Since he values my expertise in the golf markets, he asked me to call it, especially to offer a view on Els, once a blue-chip invest-ment who was widely thought to be 'gone' after blowing two tournaments recently by putting it in the water on the last hole. Fanning fancied a bet on Calcavecchia, not Els, and I confirmed to him that there were serious doubts about Els, but that maybe having blown it twice he wouldn't blow it a third time.

So with seven holes to play, Fanning had the bet on Calcavecchia anyway, and then completely forgot to watch the unfolding catastrophe on Setanta. I, meanwhile, who had had no intention of entering this market, perused the prices and saw that Els was Evens, leading by a shot with five holes to play. I made my move.

I watched Ernie somehow negotiating an awful lot of water over the last five holes, and winning by a shot, while Fanning found out the next morning that Calcavecchia had failed him. He had found the water on the sixteenth.

It is such unhappy events that are driving today's annual

statement from Paddy Power, with profits up to 72.1 million euros, partly due to 'favourable sporting results'.

It is such unhappy events that make men mad.

10 March 2008

● 5 on Murray to beat Federer @ 3/1 – **Win**

● 50 on Murray to beat Davydenko @ 5/6 – **Lose**

⚽ 30 on Man Utd to beat Lyon @ 2/5 – **Win**

● 70 on Nadal to beat Roddick @ 4/7 – **Lose**

⚽ 50 on Chelsea to beat Olympiacos @ 2/7 – **Win**

⚑ 20 on O'Meara in three-ball @ 10/11 – **Win**

⚑ 30 on Weekley in three-ball @ 11/10 – **Lose**

⚽ 75 on Barcelona to beat Villarreal @ 1/2 – **Lose**

⚽ 30 on Man Utd to beat Portsmouth @ 1/3 – **Lose**

⚑ 45 on Dyson to win Malaysia Open @ 1/2 in-running – **Lose**

. . . +65

With Man Utd losing to Portsmouth, and Chelsea losing to Barnsley, and Arsenal drawing with Wigan, the 'favourable sporting results' are piling high. Though there was a punter in Belfast who had all four winners of the FA Cup quarter-finals in an accumulator, at a rollover price of 1187/1. Sadly, it was a 10p accumulator, which meant that he won less than 120 quid for his once-in-a-lifetime inspiration. He acknowledged that it was 'a missed opportunity'.

Indeed.

But then it wasn't the sort of bet that could persuade any sane person to part with more than 10p, was it?

There was carnage too the previous weekend, when Arsenal's draw with Aston Villa resulted in 10,000 accumulators doing down.

But at least for a few minutes they all had a chance, unlike this American woman who is suing a casino for her gambling losses. She happens to be a lawyer as well as a compulsive gambler who managed to lose about a million dollars at the gaming tables of Atlantic City. She says she was given the full high-roller limousine treatment and was even allowed to have her dog Sacha at the table with her.

She gambled incessantly without eating or sleeping, and brushed her teeth with disposable wipes. And perhaps she even brushed Sacha's teeth too.

She says that no one in their right mind would keep gambling like this for five days and five nights, so clearly she was not in her right mind, therefore the casino was failing in its duty of care.

Personally, I feel that I am failing in my duty of care in the light of some of the above results.

But I'm coming to that.

These lawsuits from gamblers with catastrophic losses are obviously doomed. The addiction industry may be rampant, especially in America, but the law still doesn't give a fuck about how you acquired your vices, nor does it expect bookies or casino owners to save you from yourself.

In fact, bookies will privately admit that despite all their public protestations that they don't want to be dealing with compulsive gamblers, a couple of high-rolling addicts can make the difference between a good week and a bad week. So they need each other. And the law leaves them to it, which is probably just about right.

Generally you don't want John Q. Law getting stuck into the

betting trade, because if he decides in his wisdom that there is some 'duty of care', some sense of responsibility required on all sides, he may also decide that this thing of ours, this gambling, is so inherently irresponsible it should be suppressed altogether, and simply handed over once and for all to the excellent fellows of the organized crime sector.

Lest we forget, internet gambling may be a global phenomenon, but not in France, or Holland, or Germany, or the United States – an odd echo here, in Christian America, of the Islamic hatred of punting.

Yes there are many, many things that are against Islamic law, but apparently gambling displeases the Islamists more than just about anything else. Which is probably why all those rich Arabs had to go to such lengths to have a bet, sometimes taking over the top floor of a London betting office where they could spend the day punting serious money on the horses, unseen by the unclean ones in the shop below.

But we must not resort to easy scorn, as we grapple with the complexities of Islam.

At the start I asserted that two of the great forces of our time are radical Islam and online gambling. And their power runs deeper than the superficial similarities such as their use of the internet, and their irresistible appeal to young male obsessives with their ecstatic visions of paradise, be it one hundred virgins waiting in the next world or one hundred grand waiting in William Hill.

So as we try to understand the Christian urge to gamble, we will also try to understand the Islamic abhorrence of it, at least in their theological vision of the world.

But for the moment, in our imperfect world, we humbly suggest that the law, be it the law of God or the law of Man, is best left out of these ancient arrangements between bookie and punter. John Q. Law has a part to play in directing the traffic at a Bank Holiday meeting, or dealing with a bomb scare before the first race, or perhaps baton-charging a group of animal rights protesters who are holding up the start of the Grand National, but otherwise in this context he is generally unhelpful.

So we should be grateful that when an addict comes before the judge, the judge does not propose any remedy except perhaps some community service if you've defrauded friends and relations and whoever else you need to defraud.

You will hear these addicts described as hopeless cases – the wrong word there, because it is hope, after all, that has largely brought them to this, and if anything these forlorn cases demonstrate that they still have hope, in toxic quantities.

They will lose one more time. But they are creating bad publicity for an industry that is obsessively cultivating its image as a provider of 'fun'. And as such they are bringing some truth into the game.

I, too, am seeking the truth. To some extent this diary is about the pursuit of money, but it is ultimately about pursuit of the truth, and the wisdom we may derive from it.

The full truth is missing in the above list, because some of these losses were sustained on the international tennis circuit in matches I will not mention, because again I do not believe those results.

Gambling is now doing to tennis what drugs have been doing to athletics – destroying the concept of fair play for certain competitors, but most importantly for the punter.

I believe this particularly in the light of my relative success on the tennis courts over the last two seasons, before the game started to get away from me. In fact most tennis players to me were cash machines, in the legitimate sense. If I was suffering in any other area of my punting, I would go back to what I knew best, and take solace in the tennis, with the points racking up one after the other on the ATP website, knowing that a small but reliable income was virtually guaranteed.

Now, after these latest reverses, I have sworn off all tennis apart from the Masters Series and Grand Slam events where one assumes that most of them at least are trying – though one will still keep an eye out for our old friend 'unusual betting patterns'.

In this dark context, I am probably doing well to be still ahead. But I must take personal responsibility for some of these losses.

I take no responsibility at all for Barcelona losing at home, the second time in a week they have done me, the fuckers. And I can only smile wryly at that paltry fiver on Andy Murray to beat Federer at 3/1, a superb call, but a cruel example of a winner from which I derived the minimum benefit.

From Man Utd's home defeat to Portsmouth I derived the benefit of Man Utd losing at home to Portsmouth, and I must take responsibility for this amateurish attitude, this business of backing some hated rival in order to put 'the Indian sign' on them, and to take at least some small comfort if they win.

I was messing there, I hold my hands up.

And in the interests of transparency I should state that I am partial to this form of voodoo, to betting on things not necessarily because I want to make money but for emotional reasons, such as the notion that my involvement will in some way redound to the benefit of Liverpool Football Club, which I love.

Typically, this might involve Liverpool being held to a 0–0 draw by Wigan. It is twenty minutes into the second half, and there is no sign of a Liverpool goal. I am going mad with frustration. I feel that I am left with no alternative but to take personal charge of the situation, to enter the contest and work my magic.

I go to the 'in-running' market. I have, say, 50 on The Draw.

Here the internet gives us so many new options, for good or ill. It feels essentially different to a betting office, where you would never allow yourself to do such a thing. A betting office feels like a place of grim business, whereas the online facility feels more like a palace of varieties. And of course the technology that allows you to bet 'in-running' might well be what the internet was made for, in its purest form.

Therefore I back The Draw, because of course The Draw is what I don't want, as a Liverpool fan. So what I am bringing to the party here is my proven track record of losing. I am hoping that the gods will note my bet, as they invariably do, and decide immediately that there must be another outcome, that Liverpool must score, which of course means that I will lose the bet, but I will not care, because I will be so happy that Liverpool have scored, and are going to win the game. (It is also possible that the gods will decree a goal for Wigan, and they can be that brutal sometimes, but I don't want to think about that.)

In fairness to myself, I don't think I should be counting these as actual losses, because they are one step beyond the normal range of superstitions that afflict the punter – if 'normal' is the right word to describe the fantastical inner life of the person who seeks to influence a result by arranging the furniture in his front room in Ballina in such a way that it changes a game taking place in Bucharest; or who eats a bowl of muesli before the Merseyside Derby because it worked so well last year.

These actions are at once risible and utterly poignant.

At one level, the punter is being madly egocentric to think

that he can change something that is happening 500 miles away by changing his half-time biscuits from ginger nuts to milkchoc Goldgrain, or by poking the fire whenever the referee awards an indirect free kick. He is placing himself at the centre of the universe, the *primum mobile* who can influence all things by the smallest gesture. And yet he is also calling to mind the fearful sacraments of our most primitive ancestors, who felt so overwhelmed by the forces ranged against them yet who would still seek to gain the favour of these unseen powers with their burnt offerings.

Thousands of years later, this is where we are at.

We are like the Romans in Shakespeare's *Julius Caesar* with their portents and their great signs and their reading of the entrails. They too must have felt that they were way ahead of their savage ancestors, yet for all the genius that had enabled them to rule the world they were still listening to the gibberish of soothsayers.

And we are like them, with our most advanced technology bringing us all the way back there, to a world of garbled superstition, betting 'in-running' on Blackburn to lose to Arsenal, in the hope that Blackburn will equalize and take two points from Arsenal, which will be good for Liverpool.

God help us, but we struggle in this life.

We are tormented.

But it does not mean we are entirely stupid, just human. Maybe too human.

And it happens to the best of us. I believe that Peter Cook used to do something similar in relation to his beloved Spurs, backing them to lose so that he would always have some consolation at the end of the day.

I guess this devotion to heathen ways is another factor contributing to the abhorrence which genuinely God-fearing and good-living people have towards gambling. It helps us to understand why it is against Islamic law.

For what is the punter doing here but squandering what might be called his spiritual energies? Yes, he's squandering his money, and perhaps his wife's money, and his children's money, and maybe even somebody else's money, and that is bad. But worse, he is also squandering whatever inclinations he might have towards the mystical side of life, in its more exalted sense.

The time a man should rightly be spending in contemplation of the Prophet is wasted in contemplation of which trousers to wear to help the Hammers to victory against Everton. He is, as they say, worshipping false gods.

So as I go along, I will neither subtract my 'voodoo' losses nor add my 'voodoo' winnings to the overall figure in this account.

But historical trends tell me that the old voodoo will have cost me a few hundred by the time we're finished.

Still, I include that Man Utd defeat in the current tally because it was in the Cup, which doesn't really exercise me any more, on any level. It was still a dubious indulgence.

But the loss on Simon Dyson in the Malaysian Open was criminally negligent, and deeply sad, a clear abandonment of my duty of care. I had intended to have one bet that day, the silver bullet, Everton to beat Sunderland. Not for superstitious reasons, but because I really thought Everton would beat Sunderland. But when I went into the markets I saw there was free money to be had on Dyson with a few holes to play, and like a clown I went for it.

We often hear this sort of thing described as a loss of discipline, though I have always doubted if 'discipline' is an appropriate word to use in a gambling environment. Certainly punters are aware of certain disciplines which they set for themselves – on page one of the horse-players' manual there are ancient mantras about never backing a two-year-old the first time out, and always backing the outsider in a three-horse race. And on page one of my manual there's an iron rule that you never in any circumstances have a bet on either Tottenham or Newcastle to win, lose or draw. Because they will always find a way to let you down, always.

Which doesn't mean that I never actually break that rule, it just means I can have absolutely no excuses when I break it, perhaps because the only match on my coupon on a Monday night is, say, Tottenham v Newcastle.

My own personal code of discipline would also state in bold letters on page one that I should never even think of backing a horse, and especially a dog, and yet in moments of madness I can be found wanting in this regard, as in so many other regards.

Again I think of the punter's illusion that he is General Dwight D. Eisenhower orchestrating the Normandy landings, when he is in fact more like the boys in *Saving Private Ryan* landing on the beaches – certainly they were operating under ingrained military disciplines, but in that particular context it wouldn't ultimately have much relevance to whether they lived or died.

So Dyson let me down horribly, but I let myself down too when I let this blow to my confidence put me off Everton, who inevitably won. A real six-pointer there, a swing of nearly 100 for the one dumb play.

The Dyson defeat had messed with my emotions. It had made me angry and depressed. And as it is with the booze, it is always a mistake to be betting when you're angry or depressed. At this level, you just can't make that sort of mistake.

At this level, you can't make any mistakes.

10 March 2008

A MOMENT OF SOBER REFLECTION
'MAKES RICH FAMILIES POOR, AND HUMILIATES PROUD SOULS'

DURING THE 2006 World Cup in Germany a friend of mine was in a café in Heidelberg, when the waiter, on learning that my friend was Irish, started talking to him about Irish football – about Drogheda and Finn Harps and Bray Wanderers. It quickly became clear that the waiter had developed this strange interest in Irish football not because he had happy memories of backpacking in Ireland, or because he was just strange, but because there were no World Cup matches on that day, and there wasn't much on his betting coupon except matches featuring Longford Town and the Hoops and Bohs.

Which, if he were wise, he would simply avoid.

But like so many young men – and old men too – he was not wise. And he had many empty hours stretching ahead of him, which apparently he could fill only by betting on whatever market was available, which in this case was a list of Irish football matches. He had nothing but a punt on Cobh Ramblers to get him through that German night.

And if you still find this implausible, I have two words: Portman Park.

And another word: Steepledowns.

Portman Park and Steepledowns are among the 'venues' for Virtual Racing. So if men are betting daily on horses that don't exist, running in places that don't exist, it's not much of a stretch to imagine them betting on football played by actual people,

69

even if it's happening in a faraway land of which they know nothing.

Let us pause again to consider what is happening to men.

Across the world – the secular world at least – they have found this thing that unites them at the deepest level. Since they have no god, there is this thing that gives purpose to their lives.

It is not fanciful in the least to suppose that that waiter in Heidelberg was depending almost entirely on the evening's fare at Terryland Park or Inchicore to make his day meaningful.

Yes, men are also deeply united by their love of sport in general, but their love of betting on sport has a financial as well as an emotional kick. 'It matters more when there's money on it,' as Skybet assert, with diabolical accuracy.

Like the man in Heidelberg with his coupon who needed to know about Finn Harps, there are men in Finland who, as I write, are supposed to be concentrating on their dreary work in the post office but are thinking only of some tennis match in Morocco. Men in Greece who are driving taxis in the blazing heat are making the most intense efforts to figure out the winner of a basketball game between Utah Jazz and LA Lakers.

It is enhancing their lives and is diminishing them at the same time.

Maybe they are even embracing their own doom by retreating in their multitudes into this madness, like those generations of women who were conditioned to believe that their lives could most usefully be spent in the constant pursuit and eradication of household germs. Maybe those lost women are leaving such things behind now, liberating themselves from all those invisible terrors, and it is men who are lost in a world in which they are apparently no longer needed.

Certainly the most strenuous efforts are being made to lure these freed women into the maw of internet 'gaming' – through cards and the manifest evil of bingo – but the men got there first. In our chosen subject of sports betting, the dominance of men will be unchallenged for a thousand years. Here, and perhaps here alone, men will rule.

Because in so many ways, they have nothing better to be doing.

Physical work is increasingly obsolete. The professions are increasingly filled with women, because girls are doing better in school – as a betting man, I'd wager that that waiter in Heidelberg is just a waiter, not some guy paying his way through college. And the relentless disparagement of men as emotional and intellectual and sexual beings has perhaps contributed to a general lowering of male self-esteem.

It is quite acceptable, in a light-hearted sort of way, to ponder the need for men at all, except as sperm donors, at a time when the internet has offered them these vast avenues of retreat into porn or gambling or just idling their lives away.

A man such as Noam Chomsky would be no friend of internet sports betting, seeing it as yet another way in which the masses are being doped and duped, tranquillized and rendered completely harmless by the forces that create these sinister amusements.

He suggests that it takes no great analytical skill to challenge the systems created by our oppressors. It's just that we prefer to use such skills to figure out what the New England Patriots will be doing next Sunday.

Then again, the man who rejects the path of political agitation in favour of punting on the Patriots is doing something that really matters to him, today, tonight. And maybe he'll get around to the concerns of Noam Chomsky tomorrow, if indeed he ever does. Alone with his console – the right word, there – he can feel at least half-alive. He can use his powers of reason, which are frowned upon elsewhere, but which may assist him here in getting a result. Now and again, he can feel like he's winning.

He can make decisions, which no one will question, even when they turn out to be horribly wrong. He can feel a kind of power, even if it's just the power to orchestrate his own destruction.

In this cautionary vein I realize that I am sounding a tad Islamic. This is because the clearest arguments against the culture of endless leisure are consistently coming from the Islamic voice. With the Christian churches more or less retiring from the field of morals and moralizing, utterly defeated, we can see the emergence of two great belief-systems, one of which looks to Mecca, and the other which looks to Mecca Bookmakers, now trading as William Hill.

And for those who take their orders directly from

the Holy Koran, these are the words of Allah: 'Satan's only desire is to create among you enmity and hatred by means of intoxicants and gambling, to stop you from praying and remembering Allah.' And then the hard question: 'Will you not then stop?'

Undoubtedly there is a fundamental conflict between the gambling man and his Higher Power, whomsoever that might be. Because the gambler is setting himself up as a prophet, of sorts. He is endeavouring to arrange his own destiny. He is purporting to know what is going to happen, to second-guess the One Supreme Being who alone knows what is going to happen, and who will clearly take a dim view of some punter venturing into this area for pleasure and profit.

And one could hardly dispute the assertion from an Islamic source that gambling 'makes rich families poor, and humiliates proud souls'. Indeed if we didn't know better, we would imagine that the Prophet himself must have seen a few reverse forecasts going down, to show such perspicacity.

So the Islamist male, with all his prayer and his fasting, must be in a good place by comparison with the white Western male in his sloth and his dissipation. As they say at the poker table, he must be living right?

Well, actually, no, that's not the impression we're getting. From what we can glean, the young Islamist male is not living right at all. He has the awful intensity of those who take religion too literally, and in his more radical moments he is a danger to himself and to everyone around him.

> Will he not then stop?
>
> Certainly he seems to need more balance in his life, in the pursuit of which he could do worse than to spend an afternoon or two at Mecca Bookmakers – now trading as William Hill – just to witness the genuine suffering of the enemy, to know what Allah means when he speaks of the humiliation of proud souls.
>
> Men are men, in the end, regardless of what they worship. Men are men, and be they addicted punters or the most radical Islamists, they're looking for roughly the same thing.
>
> They want a short-cut to paradise.

11 March 2008 – Cheltenham starts today

It is ten in the morning and my intention is to make one blue-chip investment for the four days, a bet of 150 on Ruby Walsh at Evens to be leading jockey. By lunchtime I may have changed my position and decided to have a few 'nibbles', the big-time atmosphere and all the fine bullshit making me lose control.

I can only pray for a favourable outcome to these fierce internal struggles, the sort of thing Yeats meant when he said, from the debate with others we make rhetoric, but from the debate with ourselves we make poetry . . . and maybe a few quid on the side. And the Ruby debate illustrates one of the great themes I am exploring here.

Last Sunday a newspaper tipster wrote that Ruby is 'by far the most probable victor, but that price looks like a lay rather than a bet'. The tipster is looking for 'value', I am looking for 'by far the most probable victor'. And of course a bet on Ruby is primarily a bet on a human being rather than a horse – at least no specific horse. Which helps to steady the nerves.

Ah, but there is nothing like Cheltenham to bring you back to the horses, where it all began.

Cheltenham is a seminal event in most of our betting lives, especially those of us known generically as Paddy. Falling as it does around St Patrick's Day, it has become the de facto national holiday for Paddy, the antidote to all the official bullshit which involves no pleasure for Paddy, only pain, all that parading and religious observance – it was Brendan Behan who remarked that Ireland in his day was the only country in the world in which the pubs were closed at fiesta time.

So Cheltenham can partly be seen as Paddy's most ingenious creation, a celebration of his Irishness which just happens to take place in another country, and which involves all the things he likes, such as drinking and gambling and watching English sport on the TV.

And there is a special time, in the hour before the first race at Cheltenham, when Paddy is in a state of almost perfect happiness. For weeks he has been getting himself ready for this, going to Cheltenham nights in big country hotels to hear the jockeys and the trainers on the stage in the ballroom, talking about their prospects. For weeks Paddy has been building up his ammunition, getting the old butterflies, feeling that frisson in his bowels, and now it is about to start.

Now he is pumped full of hope, in a state of maximum anticipation. He is on a high, undiluted by reality. In fifteen minutes he will encounter reality, when the result of the first race is known and it is not the right result.

But right now, the hour before it all kicks off, is Paddy's golden hour. He will watch his fellow Paddies, most of them multi-millionaires, bucklepping around the winners' enclosure, pretending that they are still mad fellas who live in digs in Cricklewood. He will drink to the fine-ness of the Irish horse and the Irish jockey. And since most of the best National Hunt jockeys are Irish, this will mean quite a lot of drinking.

But the best of the best is Ruby Walsh.

Paddy loves Ruby.

It is no exaggeration to describe the punter's feelings towards a winning jockey as one of love. When Ruby drives another one up the hill, first past the post, with Paddy's money on it, love is probably a mild description of the feelings running wild inside Paddy's breast – inside the breast of any punter, if truth be told.

The endorphins are flowing, released after all the tension of the race. Paddy has been feeling the tension, has been ravaged by it, and he loves Ruby all the more because he marvels at how Ruby has somehow stayed calm, and stayed on board that horse for such a long and terrible time.

Within Paddy there is a deep restlessness of the soul. Which further explains his veneration of Ruby or any of the great Irish 'pilots' for that matter, who are like Paddy in every way except for this weird sang-froid which they possess when they get up on a horse. No matter how hysterical it gets for Paddy, he knows that Ruby is as solid as a rock.

I am Paddy. And upon that rock I have built my church.

I am Paddy, and I have known all those feelings for most of my life.

Yet today, even the high-class racing at Cheltenham can't budge me from the agonizingly hard-won conclusion that betting on horses is inherently foolish. I have grown.

Or perhaps I have just been utterly defeated.

But perhaps I too will succumb to this foolishness when the blood is up, the sportsman in me conquering the canny investor.

Indeed I like to think that the internet betting shows this side of my character, that I have always been a sportsman first, and a gambler second and third and fourth. That it is the deep pleasure of being able to enjoy so many of the world's great sporting events on TV (a massive Aussie Rules match in the middle of the night, perhaps) with just a little bet 'in-running' on the side, 'to have an interest', which attracts me to the internet providers.

After all, I spurn their poker and all that casino bullshit. I have always been completely immune to the attraction of cards and roulette, anything played on a table covered in green baize and presided over by a shady lady.

One of the first summer jobs I had was giving out the change in an amusement arcade, which cured me completely of that childhood slot-machine addiction.

At this point the addiction therapist might lapse into one of those meaningful silences, because what I am doing here has echoes of something I recognize in people with unresolved drink problems. What they do is talk about all the drinking they *don't* do. Clearly they have established some imaginary standard in their head of what constitutes an alcoholic, and, as they describe it, they will never get there. Hell, they will never even go close.

Yet the therapist giving it the silent treatment will be wondering why they're making these protestations of innocence at all, if they have no problem? You never hear some genuinely problem-free drinker scuttering on like this, pointing out that he never drinks in the afternoon or he never drinks alone or he never drinks this or he never drinks that.

I say I am in it for the sport and not just the gambling, but the head specialist will direct me towards my willingness to bet on a general election, or the Eurovision, or the final night of *Celebrity Big Brother*. Where is the sport in that?

I would argue that, in their way, these are blood sports.

So I'd be watching Cheltenham anyway, as a sportsman. Or maybe some of that Danish women's handball, in the afternoon on Eurosport.

It's all good.

A Bit of Previous
IMAGES OF MALE ANGUISH

AS A BOY, I was full of hope with my doubles and trebles and accumulators and forecasts on the Tote. I guess it was partly down to the fact that as a juvenile punter I had very little money, so the small stake rolling over into some vast accumulator had a natural appeal.

And I was stronger then.

I could take the blows. I could have two winners in a yankee and not feel too bad about all the ones that got away. These days I would be inconsolable if I won the first part of a double and suffered defeat in the second part. Inconsolable, because it's so hard to back any winner, let alone to be backing them and having them cancelled out by a subsequent loser. Sorry, I just can't take that any more.

But as a schoolboy I still remember the joyous first day at Cheltenham when I had a yankee and got just two winners up out of the four horses, one of the winners being a 10/1 shot, Good Prospect. Maybe my ecstasy was partly due to the fever, because having placed the bet at lunchtime in Power's betting office in Athlone, I cycled home and went to bed with what felt like a dose of the flu. And in my feverish cot I tuned the transistor into BBC Radio 2, to hear Peter Bromley roaring Good Prospect home. A 10/1 winner.

But a yankee being what it is, eleven bets in all, I still needed at least one other winner to get anything back. The serious money only kicked in if you got a third or a fourth winner, at which point all eleven bets, the doubles and trebles and the accumulator, came up.

I duly got a second winner that day. I guess the baleful gods could never be so cruel as to leave a child penniless with a 10/1 winner to his credit. And I made a modest profit, whereas men have built dynasties on the back of a well-chosen and well-backed 10/1 winner.

Still I persisted with the damn yankees for a long time, a 5p yankee costing 55p being my standard off-course investment product. But I think it just wore me out eventually, it was just too hard to get up the three winners you needed to make a killing. Over time I came to a deeper understanding of just how hard it is to get one winner up, let alone three or four. And over time, all that failure starts to eat away at your confidence.

You even begin to ask yourself if it's worth the trouble, because before the internet liberated us as people and as punters, you'd always have to go to a fair bit of trouble to place a bet.

Always, there were logistics involved. Obviously a trip to a race meeting was a logistical exercise in which as a youth you were entirely dependent on the whims of a grown-up, in my case usually a man called Frank. And since there was no betting office in Blackrock, at least until I grew up and became a bookie, I went to the trouble of getting a responsible adult to go to the trouble of asking a reputable Dundalk bookie if he would take a bet from me over the phone – which he did, and which worked for me on the first outing, an 11/2 winner of the Ebor Handicap at York.

It didn't work much for me after that, and eventually I would just get the bus into Dundalk and happily spend the afternoon in Charlton's SP office backing horses – a delightful way for a teenager to pass the time, but I'd still have to get the bus home, which was all very time-consuming. And time is money.

Well, actually time wasn't money back then. But it was still time.

Even during the school year in Athlone, to have a bet on the Derby I would have to swing by Power's at lunchtime on the bike, and rush my dinner as a result – yes, before online betting we had our dinner in the middle of the day.

Always, some effort would have to be made, you'd have to go out of your way somehow, simply to place a bet. When you got there, you'd invariably encounter a species close to my heart, the poor ould fellas. And as I observed in a treatise which I dedicated to those men, the offices tended to be situated down a side street in the wrong part of town. And there, in the most rudimentary conditions, you would place a bet on a horse. Or maybe a dog. But most likely a horse.

You would not be given the option of betting on who would score the first goal for the Arsenal, what the score would be at half-time and full-time, and the number of corners in the match. All that you and the poor ould fellas could do was have your bet and maybe listen to the Extel service dribbling through a battered speaker. Weirdly it was often delivered in the voice of a woman, speaking in the style of a railway announcer delivering bad news – it was probably illegal, but what the hell? Nobody cared enough to close it all down, because the respectable classes were largely unaffected by it.

Did the poor ould fellas need tea and coffee-machines and water-coolers? No, if they needed such things they could go either to a café or a bad pub. Now they have all that, the free 'still water' and the colour co-ordination, and yet they've lost something they would always want and desperately need. With the introduction of the smoking ban, they have lost the right to light up a Sweet Afton, to suck on a Harry Wragg to ease their poor nerves as they listen to the racing.

Indeed once the respectable classes had completed the job of sanitizing the betting industry, with their carpets and their toilets, it seemed almost normal not to be allowed to smoke in a betting shop, where once it would have seemed like the strangest scene imaginable.

The smoke-filled betting shop always looked right. The sight of men standing outside a betting shop smoking while the horses are inside running does not look right. And it cannot prepare you for life's

vicissitudes the way an afternoon in a smoky
gambling den could, losing and winning and losing
and losing again in the company of a bunch of poor
ould fellas and poor young fellas too, feeling their
quiet desperation along with your own.

And of course in order to partake of this unique
gaming experience, you'd have to get the cash for it,
because credit cards were not accepted in these
establishments and probably didn't exist in Ireland at
that time anyway.

Generally you got the feeling that gambling was
something that should make you suffer a bit, either
in the simple act of getting it done, or in the lack of
creature comforts in the offices, which technically
weren't supposed to even have a toilet or a television
let alone the banks of screens on the walls of today's
user-friendly joints, and the toilets which are still
regarded by many punters as being superfluous –
women need toilets, men just need to bet.

In fact some bookies are still reluctant to have a
toilet on the premises, because punters have been
known to vent their rage at some appalling injustice
by defecating on the floor. You don't hear Paddy
Power going on about this, as he spreads his message
of hope, but I am reliably informed that it is
increasingly common for punters to indulge in this
desperate act of dirty protest.

It is a very ugly scene, but I suppose it gives the
perpetrators some momentary release, some sense
that they are restoring the balance of the cosmos,
that there is justice in this world. But of course they
know in their hearts that it is a futile and vain-

glorious gesture. And being around such damaged men from an early age has probably protected me in some way.

Not only do I appreciate the fact that having a bet online is so easy, so free from logistics, I have these SP Office images of male anguish branded forever on my soul. I have seen the suffering at first hand, and smelt it, unlike the kid in his bedroom playing online poker all day and all night with his credit card, who has no such race memory, who has not seen or heard or smelt such terrible things, akin to the scenes of male torment which were such an epiphany for Nick Hornby on his first visit to Highbury.

I fear deeply for those kids who have not been exposed to these raw realities of losing. And I don't exclude my own losing here; indeed I have probably never had full closure on the St Leger of 1975 which was won by the grey Bruni, ridden by Tony Murray and trained by Captain Ryan Price, a horse I had greatly fancied but which I had to watch winning at 8/1 by about twelve lengths with none of my money on it, because I missed the bus to Dundalk.

I have had many such days, when it has not been fun. It has been the opposite of fun. To walk into a betting office with forty quid and to walk out with nothing is not a life-changing event. But if it happens more often than not, for most of your life, it induces a permanent darkening of the mind.

Back in the mid-1980s I went to the Galway Races with my father and for three days I backed losers, and nothing but losers. Twenty-one losers, none of which remotely looked like a winner at any stage. I was getting it so wrong, I wondered if I was actually going mad.

Even at the Park, which in my fonder recollections seems like an enchanted place, I may have 'gone through the card' once, but more often than not the card went through me.

So I have had my share of losing, but being near to other men as they lose is probably even more instructive, even more of a lesson in life.

In particular I recall an afternoon in a betting office in Inchicore in which a man was losing all day, losing hundreds, but still punting with the brave face, suppressing all the feelings of rage which must have been building up inside him, 'trembling inwardly', as Dostoevsky puts it, not losing the head and simply roaring in agony as he was entitled to do, a reaction which is somehow unacceptable in the unwritten code of the betting office.

It is indeed remarkable how so many of these men manage somehow to contain themselves, to confine their displays of rage to a bitter curse, or perhaps the contemptuous flinging of a losing slip into the wastepaper basket when the month's rent goes down on a dog at Perry Barr.

But they manage it somehow, as this man in Inchicore was managing it.

Even as he left the premises he was being philosophical. He even said a big smiling goodbye to everyone before he left, goodbye and let's hope for better things tomorrow. And he held himself together until he reached his car, which was parked around a corner in a place where he could not be seen by his comrades in the betting office, or so he thought. But as I left the premises I saw him sitting in the driver's seat. And he wasn't putting on the brave face any more.

He was banging his forehead off the steering wheel, again and again and again.

17 March 2008

---

150 on Walsh to be Leading Jockey at Cheltenham @ Evens – **Win**
100 on Woods to win Bay Hill Invitational @ Evens – **Win**

. . . +320

That tipster was right. Ruby was 'by far the most probable victor'. But for all practical purposes I stopped reading at that point, ignoring the second half of the sentence which read, 'but at that price he looks more of a lay than a bet'.

It was a good point well made, but for me it was just a bit too clever. Frankly I reckon it's clever enough to work out the first part, without then ignoring your own cleverness and forging ahead into another realm of advanced cleverality, where in all likelihood you will find the graveyard of many Betfair punters.

Like most of the international online betting community, I broadly welcome the arrival of Betfair, which allows the punter to be the bookie if he feels like it. This excludes the bookie in the traditional sense, leaving Paddy Power and his upper-middle-class corporate ilk out there with their humungous profits, their 'favourable sporting results' and their shit jokes.

But it doesn't necessarily make the punter's task any easier, and in some ways I believe that it complicates an already complex situation – at least it complicates it too much for a simple soul such as myself.

I am trying to construct a belief system here, one to which I can adhere with the uncomplicated fervour of a devout Muslim. And having ultimately rejected the temptation of doubles, trebles and 'accas', I am not about to be lured into the badlands of 'laying', of becoming a bookie myself as the mood takes me. Yes, when I was young I wanted to be a bookie, but it didn't happen, probably for a reason. Probably, I wouldn't have been any good at it.

Of course I'm tempted by that beguiling Betfair option of betting on horses to lose – it seems such a relief after a lifetime of thankless toil trying to get them to win – but a few celebrated court cases and tales of chicanery have taught us that even in the most capable hands that too can blow you away.

So I am a punter and a punter I will stay. Inasmuch as I can resist these many temptations, I will have individual bets, one at a time, to win. Straight, no chaser.

And I feel that this Cheltenham result gives me a certain moral standing here. That tipster called it right, and still he lost. Like most gamblers he is quite a clever guy, and like most gamblers he is undone by his own cleverality. He knows too much. Or at least he has too many options in front of him. Again, if it was in the interest of the punter to have more options, my Blue Square service would probably offer me two football matches a year in the Blue Square Premier League to bet on, and maybe the odd race at Walthamstow, and nothing else. Instead, the range of markets at my disposal is kaleidoscopic.

Tonight, for example, in the football markets alone, with a straight face I can treat myself to a choice of Besiktas v Crvena Zvezda, or Borussia Dortmund v Carl Zeiss Jena, or Rapid Vienna v Austria Vienna – could be a draw here, your local derbies tend to end in draws. And I can get into the mood with an afternoon interest in the important Indian Cricket League match between the Ahmedabad Rockets and the Mumbai Champs.

Many options there, many ways to go, in that fool's paradise.

For the guy who thought Ruby was more a lay than a bet, there was just one option too many in front of him. And technically he may have been right, but it didn't get him to where the punter needs to be, which is a place where he has more money at the end of the day than at the beginning.

Yes, the punter needs to be there, but he wants to be in other places as well. He wants to see his judgement vindicated, almost for the aesthetic pleasure of it. Which may explain further why punting is so appealing to so many men who would otherwise be considered bright.

For these men, to 'lay' Ruby would provide a deeper pleasure than the more obvious ploy of just backing him to win the damn thing – though in the end it provided no pleasure at all for them, only pain. Only pain.

So reluctantly I must walk away from Betfair, not because it is offering me too little but because it is offering me just a little bit too much.

And perhaps in this context we should also reflect on the way that first-time punters, many of them women, seem to have the most infuriating ability to back winners while we, with all our cleverality, are down the glen. Perhaps it is more than just dumb luck. Perhaps the brutish simplicity they are bringing to the game is giving them an edge. Their very ignorance is out there, working for them. What do they know of doubles, trebles and accas, of yankees, heinzes and penfolds? And how much better off are they as a result?

Still I salute the professional gambler Harry Findlay, who

loves Betfair and who became an inspirational presence in all our lives last week as the owner of Denman, facile winner of the Gold Cup. For me the remarkable thing about Findlay is not necessarily that he had a losing bet of approximately £2.5 million on New Zealand to win the Rugby World Cup (though that is indeed remarkable) but that much of his belief-system seems to coincide roughly with my own.

Unusually for a massive, massive punter, Findlay favours the short-priced winner. Like me and Derek McGovern of the *Mirror*, he believes that a winner is always welcome – unless it's Michael Winner. Success breeds success, even if it comes in very small amounts.

'Say one fellow backs 20/1 shots,' Findlay explains. 'After twenty losers, he backs a winner and he's level. Another fellow's betting Evens. After ten winners and ten losers, he's level. They've both got the same money, but he's been right ten times. Who's going to have more confidence?'

My sentiments exactly.

And the other thing we have in common, me and the great Harry Findlay, is our veneration of Tiger Woods.

After two rounds of the Bay Hill Invitational, Tiger was seven shots off the lead. And with Ruby having a slow start at Cheltenham, I was in the worrying position of having zero in my account, with my funds all tied up in depreciating assets.

Yet I bore no ill will towards Tiger. At this stage he owes me nothing. And then Ruby, the best jockey on the best horses, did what the best jockeys on the best horses will most probably do. And then Tiger found the extra gear, and the extra gear after that, which in this case involved finding a 24-foot downhill birdie putt on the last hole to win by one shot.

It is worth quoting Findlay's testimonial in an interview with Chris McGrath in the *Independent*: 'I've never met Tiger, but I know him better than anyone on the planet . . . He's so easy to read, that's the great thing about him. And Federer. Not only are they the best of all time, they speak with the greatest clarity, and the greatest honesty. There's never any ulterior motive . . . He's from somewhere else, Tiger, must be. He's the greatest human being on earth.'

22 March 2008

● 30 on Murray to beat Haas @ 4/9 – **Lose**

⌐ 25 on Mickelson in three-ball @ 8/11 – **Win**

● 30 on Jankovic to beat Davenport @ 4/7 – **Win**

⌐ 30 on Bourdy in three-ball @ 11/8 – **Lose**

⌐ 55 on Mickelson in three-ball @ 8/13 – **Lose**

● 40 on Nadal to beat Djokovic @ 6/5 – **Lose**

⌐ 150 on Woods to win WGA-CA @ 4/6 in-running – **Lose**

. . . +45

William Hill has duly won that 'self-exclusion' lawsuit taken against them by Graham '£347,000 on the Ryder Cup' Calvert. Which is probably the best for all concerned. Not least for Graham Calvert.

He loses again, but in the last few days it seems like the whole world is losing. And it is losing so much, it can never win again. Bear Stearns has gone down, and they're talking about the Fed cutting interest rates to zero, meaning that in America there will be free money.

Indeed.

There is a growing suspicion that the entire American financial system – make that the entire world financial system – is based on bullshit. And I suspect that deep down the world has known this for some time, and that this thing of ours, this global gambling phenomenon, is not unrelated.

In fact several websites offer the punter the opportunity to bet on 'financials', one of the more brainless of all markets involving nothing more than a punt on whether the FTSE or the Dow will be above or below a certain number at a certain time – a numbers racket, if you like. With the financials, instead of having some trader pissing away our life savings on the floor of the NYSE, we figure that if there's pissing away to be done, we will do it ourselves.

And with these increasingly frequent financial meltdowns, we see the terrifyingly primitive nature of these supposedly sophisticated systems. Certainly for the punter it is most alarming to hear financial analysts talking about stock markets dominated by 'feelings'. In this case feelings of fear and greed. And 'sentiment'.

Dear God, they're talking about 'sentiment' in relation to the deployment of billions of other people's money. 'Sentiment', a thing which the humble punter strives to avoid at all times, even if he's putting 20 quid on a dog in the 2.27 at Leicester. Though I do confess that my large loss on Tiger in the WGC-CA was partly based on sentiment. I wanted him to somehow keep winning every tournament, not just for me, but for the world.

You could say that Bear Stearns drove me to it. Because I am starting to see Tiger as America's symbol of hope as it enters this Great Depression. Like the Hollywood heroes who raised the spirits of the people in the 1930s and during the Second World War, Tiger is doing the same by winning every tournament in which he tees it up.

Well ... nearly every tournament. Unlike the Hollywood

heroes, Tiger just can't win them all. He is the greatest human being on earth, but he is still a human being, not an actor in his own biopic. There is no Take Two for Tiger.

But there is no bullshit either. Bush the Bullshitter Supreme started a war based entirely on bullshit; he presides over a financial system that is disintegrating because it is based entirely on bullshit. So Tiger emerges as perhaps the only American in public life for whom bullshit is not an option.

Now America turns its lonely eyes to Tiger Woods.

And despite my grievous loss on this occasion, and the world's loss, over time an investment in Tiger Woods is still the smart play. Even despite this unhappy reverse, I am still significantly ahead on the Woods account.

I can't help noting, though, that some of my old blue-chip reliables, such as Andy Murray and Rafael Nadal and Phil Mickelson, have also failed me in recent days. Again these men owe me nothing, or at least not much. But there is a chilling similarity to a previous run of losers which largely featured their names. Which reminds me that in Alcoholics Anonymous they say that doing the same thing time after time and expecting a different result is the definition of insanity. It's probably the definition of insanity in Gamblers Anonymous too.

But at least I'm still ahead, unlike Bear Stearns, though stock market analysts might point out that my gains and losses seem to be cyclical in nature, a bit like the Dow and the FTSE. That every period of prosperity seems inevitably to be followed by a downturn. And that the Irish Stock Exchange has had ten years of prosperity whereas my bull markets tend to last about ten days.

Still I maintain that I am more in control of my portfolio than the guys betting on the Hang Seng. And did I mention that I'm still ahead? Not behind?

Likewise that guy who arrived in New York with his 100 dollars would still be ahead, not behind, having glimpsed some of the vast possibilities in front of him, and vowed to absorb all the lessons of these early exchanges, absorbing the patterns which are starting to emerge.

In such a dangerous and godless world, where the most venerable institutions are going down, we can all empathize with the predicament of that man. We are all exposed to forces that we barely comprehend; we need some affirmation of our place in the universe. And this is where gambling comes in. Like the market traders with their 'sentiment', even something as technically sophisticated as online gambling brings us back to the most primitive impulses, to this need for reassurance that in a hostile world the force is with us, that we are in good standing with the baleful gods, that we are lucky.

A Bit of Previous
ADDICTION IS THE NEW SIN

OF COURSE I was gambling long before I became an alcoholic. That is, if I accept that I am indeed an alcoholic.

Put it like this: if I'm talking to some other alcoholic, or sitting in an AA room as I was wont to do about twelve years ago, just after I stopped drinking, I am not uncomfortable with that description. But in any other context, increasingly I take the view that it gives the wrong impression. The word is, as they say, unhelpful.

I am not alone in this. I note that my old drinking buddy John Waters has arrived at a similar place in his journey, after many years of sobriety.

So when Pat Kenny asked me on the *Late Late Show* last year if I was an alcoholic, I did not say 'yes'. I parried his question, because I was speaking to a large audience that was bound to contain numerous individuals with a false understanding of that condition. A false understanding which ideally they would correct by reading my novel *The Rooms*, which was the reason for my appearance on the show, and which has a main character who goes to meetings in 'the rooms' of Alcoholics Anonymous.

Since I needed to write a novel of 75,000 words to give myself a true understanding of these matters, I felt that a one-word answer on *Late Late* just wouldn't be right.

Terminology is everything here. It can determine the entire course of your life.

For example, thirty years ago the likes of me wouldn't have been regarded by anyone as an alcoholic, though at a certain stage of my life I had become 'too fond' of alcohol.

The terminology is constantly changing. But I am certain that at the time when I became 'too fond' of the drink, it was helpful to me to describe myself as an alcoholic.

I think that by taking the extreme view, by defining whatever was wrong with me in that way, I was able to do what I needed to do. Which was, basically, to stop drinking.

And not to start again for the forseeable future. Though of course we always say we are only off it for today.

And while this is an excellent example of the use of the A-word being helpful, there are many other examples of its being deeply unhelpful. At one level, it has such alarming connotations that it may prevent someone seeking help because he just can't see himself as the stereotypical 'alco' who drinks four bottles of meths a day and who lives in a cardboard box.

And at another level, there's the addiction industry, which is growing daily and which seems to be encouraging anyone who indulges in any form of vice to consider themselves addicted. Which in turn means that they will need to be treated. Which is where the addiction industry comes in.

So before I'd be calling myself an alcoholic in any context, be it in daily life or on live television, I would need to know exactly what that means. And I don't think anyone knows any more.

I don't think anyone rightly knows what an addict is either, because in my relatively short lifetime it has changed from a way of describing the junkie strung out on heroin into a word used to describe otherwise healthy people who eat too much chocolate. Or who think they eat too much chocolate. Or who have been given to believe that they eat too much chocolate, because they saw someone on a talk show describing herself as a chocoholic, and she eats less chocolate than they do.

Addiction is the new Sin, and the addiction industry is the new Church.

So in an area where words must have a definite meaning, where you really need to have a deep level of accuracy, increasingly you get the dark agendas of politics and religion. It is simply assumed, for example, that if a person is isolated from family and friends, if he has developed antisocial habits due to his drinking, he is inherently sick.

But of course this is in many ways a moral judgement, not a medical or a psychiatric one.

It represents a certain view of the world and of how men should live, which calls to mind the 'bourgeois morality' condemned by Alfred Doolittle, and which is not a million miles away from that of the old Anti-Happiness League itself. It's an attitude that has blurred the lines between an enthusiasm and an addiction in the true sense of that word, which I believe should still conjure up the image of heroin in the backstreets rather than chocolate on the sofa. If you cast the net too wide, you are saying that almost everyone is addicted to something. And if everyone is addicted, then no one is addicted.

The other night there was a programme on RTE about work/life balance in which a man who acknowledged that he works too much was said to be 'addicted' to his work. So we now have a definition of the addict which stretches from the totally feckless degenerate out of his head on 'gear', to the decent hard-working man working every hour God sends.

And that, for me, is too big a stretch.

Having said all that, I do believe that gambling, and especially online gambling, is deeply addictive, in the true sense of the word as I understand it. And sometimes I wonder if gambling in general is the most powerful of all the addictions, the purest form of addiction in that it doesn't involve you taking any substance up your nose, or drinking anything or eating anything, and it definitely doesn't involve your staying too late at the office.

The gambler can stay physically healthy for a lot longer than the drinker or the drugger. He can be down a million dollars and still look like a million dollars, so he can look in the mirror and like what he sees, and can continue to believe in himself, and others can continue to believe in him, until the very end.

But more than this, gambling is the only addiction which holds out this promise: no matter how much damage is done, you can always get back to where you started, *by indulging in the very thing that has caused the damage in the first place.*

If the heroin addict's health is not irreparably damaged, he may get back to where he started, health-wise, by going clean. But he surely won't do it by continuing to take smack. Likewise, if the alcoholic's liver is not irreparably damaged he may get back to where he started, if he stops drinking. But he surely won't do it by continuing to drink.

Gambling alone offers you a way out of the hole using the same shovel with which you dug that hole. And compared to gambling, all the other addictions offer something quite vague, some change of mood. With gambling, you can actually put a number on it.

Maybe those Islamists reserve a particular loathing for it because in their way they have always understood that gambling is the daddy of them all, the original sin. They agree with the American left-wing journalist Heywood Broun who opined that 'the urge to gamble is so universal, and its practice so pleasurable, I assume it must be evil'.

Has Islam perhaps called it right here? Has Islam always known that gambling is the hardest of all the addictions to break? Because it's about setting yourself up as a prophet. It's about having your judgement vindicated, it's about being proved right.

Given the large number of alcoholics who have won the Nobel Prize for Literature, we realize that the most intelligent of men can become hopelessly addicted to booze, but they are not necessarily using that intelligence in order to pursue their addiction – as long as they can remember where they left the bottle, the act of drinking requires no great brainpower on their part, whereas the act of gambling inherently involves some sort of an intellectual challenge.

Only slot-machines or bingo are completely brainless.

And so today I am having another of those Islamic moments, in which I see how gambling engages the terrible vanity of Man. When he is exploiting his intellect for personal gain, and taking pride in it, he also connects with his capacity for destruction, which can be limitless.

His faith in himself, and in his ability to predict the outcome of certain contests, becomes a corrupted version of the one true faith, which should involve men getting down on their knees several times a day and praying fervently to Allah for the salvation of their souls, rather than standing up in betting offices scribbling down their vision of the future, staking the security of their wife and children on it, and then, with a fervour that is all twisted, praying in entirely the wrong way for the right result.

That's how I read it anyway, and yeah, there are times when I can only look at it with Islamic eyes, Islam which has been calling it right all along.

So am I addicted to gambling? Well, it was my first enthusiasm before the drink took hold, but then I went off it for a long time, which suggests that any addiction I may have had was not that strong.

Ah, but having returned to it, am I replacing one addiction with another? Having been finally rejected in my long love affair with the drink, have I just returned to my first love?

It's an interesting question, but one to which the questioner invariably expects the answer 'yes' from a shamed addict.

I would suggest a different answer. In my case, perhaps gambling has served as an alternative therapy, which answers the need for escapism that I carry within me, and as such is probably at least as credible as any of the alternative therapies out there.

I'll listen to the therapist with her loaded definitions of Reality, disputing my version of Reality, in which I am relying for my happiness on events which are completely beyond my control. I'll listen to that, but self-diagnosis is the only kind that ultimately works in these matters, and as this process continues, I'll try to arrive at an honest conclusion.

As it stands, I would probably fulfil several of the criteria for 'compulsive gambling' that you find in those magazine questionnaires – 20 Tell Tale Signs

That You Are a Compulsive Gambler.

I believe that people enjoy doing these questionnaires, declaring themselves to be addicted, because at some level they feel it makes them more interesting. It gives them something in common with the celebrities who are willing to confess their own descent into rehab hell, because they think it makes them more interesting, and they are trying to find some excuse in the area of psychobabble for behaving like a complete arsehole. Why else would they do it?

In questionnaire terms, my level of commitment to the cause of punting would be deeply ominous. They would say that I have become psychologically dependent on it, that it plays too large a part in my life, which again disturbs me because it seems to suggest that the bozo who is compiling this survey has a better idea of how my time should be spent than I do myself.

But even in those bullshit terms, I have always failed the most obvious test, in that I have never lost a significant amount of money gambling, or had a bet with money I couldn't afford to lose. But I know too much about addiction in the true sense simply to rule myself out of the running because of the financial aspect. As Edward G. Robinson put it, talking about poker in *The Cincinnati Kid*, 'money is just a tool in this game, as language is to thought'.

As this journey unfolds, I may arrive at the conclusion that I am addicted to online gambling, up to a point. But can you be addicted to anything 'up to a point'?

Ultimately, despite the emotional and psychological factors, I believe that the best way to assess a man's gambling habits is to follow the money. For example, if I start losing substantial amounts of money here, obviously I will be obliged to review the situation.

Perhaps if I look at the glass half-empty, I see myself as the equivalent of the 'controlled drinker', the man who may have addiction issues, but who drinks in such a way that he somehow stays on the right side of the line – albeit at such a cost in terms of the sheer physical and emotional effort that he is damaged by it anyway.

And the 'controlled drinker' invariably gets out of control from time to time, even if he does it in secret in a securely locked hotel room.

In that context I am a 'controlled gambler', who has never been out of control . . . except . . . perhaps one day back in 1994 when José Maria Olazábal won the Masters. Being otherwise engaged, I had asked a friend to have £20 for me on Olazábal to win the Masters, and the friend forgot about it, and Olazábal won at 14/1.

Except for that . . . I have been totally . . . totally in control.

And even if I reluctantly decide to give this a bad name, to say that I am 'addicted' up to a point, it raises perhaps the best question of them all:

So what?

30 March 2008

- 20 on Earth Mover @ 8/15 – **Lose**
- 30 on England (draw no bet) to beat France @ 11/10 – **Lose**
- 25 on York City to beat Northwich Victoria @ 8/11 – **Lose**
- 170 on Murphy to beat Harold @ 2/7 – **Win**
- 10 on Bradley to beat Ohio @ 10/11 – **Win**
- 20 on Carter to beat Bingham @ 4/7 – **Win**
- 10 on Murphy to beat Junhui @ 5/6 – **Win**
- 65 on Murphy to beat Allen @ 8/15 – **Win**
- 25 on Arsenal to beat Bolton @ 8/11 – **Win**
- 40 on Ochoa in three-ball @ 8/13 – **Win**
- 40 on Ochoa to win Safeway tournament @ 6/4 – **Win**
- 70 lost on tennis matches in suspicious circumstances

. . . +120

A close analysis reveals that for legal reasons I have again omitted to name several losers on the tennis courts. But I have subtracted these losses from the bottom line because I tend to agree with Count Leo Tolstoy who said that a gentleman is someone who pays his gambling debts, even when he knows he has been cheated.

I'll give the game of tennis another shot at redemption, by having 100 on Federer at 5/6 to win the Miami Masters tournament, the Fed being presumably above suspicion, and, like Tiger, a superman. But from now on I'll try to confine my tennis betting to the French Open and Wimbledon, and I'll await further stories of match-fixing, perhaps even a tribunal of inquiry in which I am willing to make a Victim Impact Statement.

It's also noteworthy that I had my largest bet so far – 170 on snooker's Shaun Murphy in the China Open, in which defeat would have reduced me to zero. But to my eternal shame I succumbed to the Monday Night Football on Setanta, losing deservedly on York City against Northwich Bleeding Victoria. Yes, maybe I am addicted, up to a point.

And I take no pleasure either in admitting that I bet on England in a friendly, to win or to draw – naturally, they lost.

Heartwarmingly, the Tigress came good for me again. Lorena Ochoa won by six shots this time, and now we arrive at a very interesting point. It has occurred to me that if you took away all the other bets, leaving just the ones on the Tiger and the Tigress, you would arrive at roughly the same figure, the same profit margin. In real terms, all the other bets have amounted to zero, nothing gained and nothing lost. Which isn't bad actually, as in less capable hands they might have amounted to a lot less than zero.

But there is much food for thought here.

Only by a superhuman effort have I broken even on betting without the Tiger and Ochoa. Yet I also see the day-to-day involvement as an educational tool, a bit like that spokesman for Betfair who recently described the insane market on the Republic of Ireland manager job as something which had at least one positive aspect – by introducing a lot of people to the ways of Betfair, it served as 'an educational tool'.

And while there are some who might question its value to society in general, I also see this diary serving as an educational tool, albeit one which benefits the punter, rather than inveigling him further into the abyss.

It is distinctly possible that if I bet on nothing else this year apart from Tiger Woods and Lorena Ochoa, I will make a decent profit. If I bet large enough, I will make a lot more than a decent profit. There is, however, a slight structural flaw in this proposition. At most, this would mean having one bet a week, perhaps one a fortnight.

You can bet on a horse or a dog twenty or thirty times a day. And with the dogs you know your fate in about thirty seconds – a time scheme which undoubtedly favours the bookie, otherwise it would not have been his modus operandi since time immemorial.

With these winning bets on Tiger and Ochoa, I have had to wait four days for the result – though Ochoa has effectively got it done in three, and even two days. Still, it's a long time.

From one perspective, you're getting a bang for your buck with the four-day event. Trouble is, as a punter you tend to prefer a series of small bangs, rather than the one big bang, for your buck. Sadly, that's the way the bookie likes it too. The punter craves action, every day, in every way, and he just can't get it when his funds are tied up for days.

Yet, just because all that betting of mine has yielded a return of absolute zero, it doesn't mean it has all been in vain. On the contrary, I have had plenty of what Paddy Power risibly calls 'fun' – and incidentally, when they're talking about these 'fun bets', they always talk about bets on who'll be the first to score, or who'll score the next goal, which are just magnets for mugs.

Still, even by these debased standards, I have had 'fun'.

I have also had a ringside seat at some of the world's great sporting events, and some of the world's worst, and it has cost me precisely nothing. Indeed it has arguably honed my instincts for the bigger plays, which have moved me ahead, meaning that Blue Square has been paying me a small fee for the privilege of having me using their excellent services.

And its effectiveness as an educational tool can be seen in the clear pattern that is now emerging. Clearly I can continue around-the-houses, as it were, betting most days on whatever takes my fancy, as long as I know that I am highly unlikely to do anything better than break even. But if I'm wise, I'll somehow restrain myself, and keep my ammunition for the big stuff.

Am I ready for that yet? Probably not.

Probably I am still a slave to my human weaknesses, but perhaps by the time I reach Valhalla in September, I will have become a better punter in a fundamental sense, indeed a better person all round.

Because, being weak, when we bet most of us aren't looking for money, as such; we're just looking for money to bet with. We're always reinvesting, always giving something back, but hopefully reaching the level I have achieved after about two months of this exercise, whereby I am betting with the bookies' money.

As regards an actual return on investment, a friend described it best when I asked him what he had got out of his betting in material terms over the last year. He thought about it for a long time, and then he replied, wistfully: 'A pair of shoes.'

He added that this was due to a symbolic, once-off withdrawal, after a remarkable win, and that otherwise in shoe terms the money he had lost could have kept the cast of *Sex And The City* in Manolo's.

And one more thing, which illustrates how hard it is to become a better punter, and a better person.

The first transaction listed above is a bet on a horse in an average race at Fairyhouse. I did this in guilt and in shame, against all my own protestations that betting on horses is inherently foolish, and especially so in average races. But I should add that not only was Earth Mover an odds-on shot which lost, there was only one other horse in that race.

Oh, the things that I have seen, on the trail of the great white buffalo . . .

7 April 2008

- 25 on Ochoa to win two-ball @ 1/2 – **Win**
- 100 on Federer to win Miami Masters @ 5/6 – **Lose**
- 40 on Mickelson in three-ball @ 4/6 – **Win**
- 110 on Scott to win Shell Open @ 15/8 – **Lose**
- 160 on Portsmouth to win FA Cup @ 5/6 – **Unsettled**
- 60 on Gloucester to beat Munster @ 10/11 – **Lose**
- 60 on Nadal to beat Davydenko @ 4/9 – **Lose**
- 55 on Bourdy to win Estoril Open in-running @ 1/2 – **Win**

. . . –100

As Thomas Paine put it, no doubt after a poor run of form at Coral's, there are the times that try men's souls.

I'm back where I started after taking a few wrong turns – a combination of extreme negligence and bad luck. Both, in the case of Adam Scott, who shot 9-under in the first round and then withdrew from the Shell Open with a strep throat, for Christ's sake.

Federer and Nadal losing in the same week should bring the final curtain down on my brief and sordid love-affair with tennis – but it probably won't, because it must come under the heading of bad luck, and at least they were trying.

Betting on rugby deserves no luck, is worse than negligent, and is a contemptible business all round. And negligence was also clear in a couple of bets that didn't happen – having demanded one miracle too many from Tiger, I backed off Ochoa in the Kraft Nabisco tournament – which she won, of course.

I would have won big on Arsenal and Liverpool to draw,

except I neglected to notice that it was a noon kick-off. I can only console myself with the thought that the true punter would never make such a mistake. I think of Stan Bowles, the old QPR wizard who has always enjoyed a punt, and who tends to be a stickler for punctuality. Stan Bowles might be a lot richer these days had he been just a little more tardy over the years on his way to the office.

But I am a tad disturbed too, by the place in which I find myself. Yes, it's roughly where I started, but it has become a somewhat more dangerous place in the meantime.

Eagle-eyed readers will note that the bets are getting a bit bigger. I can't rightly explain this; perhaps it's just the intensity of the campaign, and of this diary, pumping up my need for action. They are still not big by any standard, but they are undoubtedly bigger. Which the addiction 'expert' would recognize as the classic pattern, and which might suggest to a less resilient type that we are on the slippery slope.

And I am indulging for the first time in what might be called 'creative accounting'. This involved the 'unsettled' bet on Portsmouth, whom I backed at the semi-final stage to win the FA Cup. Quite rightly, I have not counted the stake of 160 as a loss. But since Portsmouth won at the weekend and are now in the final with a massive, massive chance of winning, I am committing what may be a cardinal sin in the eyes of the baleful gods, by counting my 'winnings' in advance.

I realize the risks, but I'm doing it anyway, because it just makes me feel better.

Perhaps, on a microscopic level, I am gaining an insight into the mind of a Jérôme Kerviel or even a Nick Leeson, when they assumed that in all likelihood certain moneys would be arriving very soon, and everything would be all right on the night, only to discover that life is not like that.

These reverses have also come at a bad time, as I am planning a major punt on Tiger for the Masters. Which is a perfectly sensible thing to do, except I want to have more than 100 on him. In fact I want to have 400 on him. So do I go back to the well for another 300?

I think I understand a little of what a man feels when he starts drifting into deeper waters. Because when I contemplated throwing another 300 or even 500 into the pot for Tiger, I was reassured by this thought: I have the money. I can make another successful deposit with the click of a button and it will make bugger-all difference to my life, or those of my beloved wife and children.

And what is so strange about this thought?

What is strange is the word 'reassured'.

Because when a man goes back to the well, he should not be 'reassured'. He should speculate that he might find himself going back to the well again if Tiger somehow can't win the Masters. And if he is operating mainly on the basis that he 'has the money', and there's plenty more where that came from, so that's all right then, at what point does it cease to be all right? Is there in fact any such point?

These days, in theory and therefore in practice, you can arrange it so that you will always 'have the money', there will always be plenty more where that came from, almost until they drag you off to the proverbial debtors' prison – without the proverbial.

In fact if I make a successful deposit into my Blue Square account of four grand off my credit card to bet on Tiger, I will still have about six grand of magic Visa money with which to make other successful deposits. Which is also reassuring.

Though in reality I am not dealing here with four or six grand, but with genuinely small sums of money, I feel I am gaining a genuine insight into 'the slippery slope' and how it works.

When this new dynamic arrives, always unannounced, it brings a strange sort of light-heartedness in the face of catastrophe. You may have lost a shed-load of money, but now that it's done, well . . . it wasn't so bad, was it? It is only money, after all, it is only money. Nobody died, after all. Nobody died.

As long as you have reasonably easy access to reasonably large sums of money, as a punter you feel there is always a way out. You wouldn't quite call this feeling a nice warm glow, or a peaceful easy feeling, but it is still perversely a source of some comfort.

And with no sign of your apparently endless supplies of hope running out either, you can continue to draw on that source of comfort, in increasingly large amounts.

Yes, this tends to be another anomaly of the punting life: as resources become scarcer, you make heavier demands on them. And you find yourself in this topsy-turvy situation, essentially, because you are losing your mind.

You don't know it, but that's the way it is when you're losing your mind. Otherwise it wouldn't happen to some of the brightest men of their generation.

Perhaps you're just asking too much of your powers of reason, trying to work out the winner of a tennis match these days. Whatever it is, your reason sort of wears out under all the strain. You start losing it, and at some mysterious point you lose it completely, and there is no way back. What is this mysterious point?

I don't believe I'm close to it. But I do believe it is never very far away. Which doesn't seem to make much sense, but if it did it wouldn't be mysterious.

Unfortunately we only get a clearer idea of that point in retrospect. Jérôme Kerviel, in retrospect, may be starting to realize the moment when he touched that point, but when it was happening to him he was incapable of seeing it. In fact it must have seemed absurd to him, simply to stop when he was, maybe, just the one billion behind. And at three, four, five billion behind, he had moved to a parallel universe from which no man can return.

It was a mystery which fascinated Dostoevsky in his classic *The Gambler*. His game was roulette, but his descriptions of the feverish state of the gambler have an eerie resonance. When the fever takes hold, according to Dostoevsky, all that is left are 'glimmerings of reason'.

He writes: 'When, on my way to the gaming room, I hear from two rooms away the chink of the coins pouring out of the scoops, I am thrown into a ferment.' Once started on that path, according to Dostoevsky, 'it is like sliding down a toboggan run on a sledge, going faster and faster all the time'.

Yes, Dostoevsky knew how unhinged a man can become in this punting game.

His main character is chided thus: 'you've become insensible. You've not only renounced life, your own interests and those of society, your duty as a man and a citizen, your friends (and you did have them, all the same) – you've not only renounced every aim whatever in life, except winning at roulette – you have even renounced your memories. I remember you at a passionate and intense period in your life; but I am sure you have forgotten all the best influences of that time; your dreams, your most urgent present desires, go no further than pair et impair, rouge, noir, the middle dozen numbers, and so on, I'm convinced of it!'

Ah, but the accused answers him thus: 'Let me tell you I've

forgotten nothing at all. I've only driven it all out of my head, even my memories, for the time being, until I have radically altered my circumstances ... then ... then, you will see, I shall rise from the dead!'

He is trying to 'find a man within myself, before he vanishes for good!'

And Dostoevsky leaves us with the defiant gambler vowing to rise again. 'Yes! I have only to be prudent and patient for once in my life – and that's all!' he raves.

I have only to stand firm once, and I can change the whole course of my destiny in an hour!

The chief thing is strength of will. I need only remember the incident of this sort seven months ago at Roulettenburg, before my final ruin. Oh, it was a remarkable case of determination: I had lost everything then, everything ... As I was going out of the station I looked – and there in my waistcoat pocket was one surviving gulden. 'Ah, so I shall be able to have dinner!' I thought, but when I had walked about a hundred paces I changed my mind and went back. I staked that gulden on manqué (that time it was manqué) and there really is something special in the feeling when, alone, in a strange country far away from home and friends, not knowing what you will eat that day, you stake your last gulden, your very, very last! I won, and twenty minutes later I left the station with 170 gulden in my pocket. That is a fact! You see what one's last gulden may sometimes mean! And what if I had lost courage then, if I had not dared to decide! Tomorrow, tomorrow it will all come to an end!

A Bit of Previous
'I HAD DARED TO RUN THE RISK! AND NOW I WAS A MAN AGAIN!'

AT THIS STAGE it might have occurred to certain parties in the addiction industry that there seems to be almost no mention in this diary of my loved ones, and of daily life down here in Avoca.

They might note that I am living with my wife and daughter in a lovely place, in the place where they shot *Ballykissangel* itself, but instead of a rural diary something along the lines of *A Year In Provence*, apparently I see nothing to excite me or to inspire my pen except Monday Night Football on Setanta and Betting In-Running.

On noting this, certain parties might purse their lips knowingly. They might want something a bit more 'holistic' from a man who wakes up every morning in one of the most beautiful places on earth.

They might be using words like 'isolated' to describe my state of mind. And 'isolated' is bad. The man who is 'isolated' is not living in a 'holistic' way. And he is a long way down the road to being 'addicted'.

To which I would reply that this is an inherently foolish point of view. Betting in the old-fashioned way in the SP office had its moments of group con-sciousness, but internet betting does not in any way draw you into the local community. It is not a nice thing, like strolling along a country lane and dropping in to some local farmer who makes his own cheese. In a holistic way.

So I guess it is my thing, and my thing alone. And I wouldn't include it as an intrinsic part of our County Wicklow idyll if I was doing 'A Life In The Day' for the Sunday supplement. It is a vice, like smoking or drinking.

But if you deduce from this that I am 'isolated', I suggest you are introducing an agenda of a deeply dubious kind. You will also be using words like 'detached' to describe my state of mind, another of those words put out there by the addiction industry to make good people feel bad about themselves. Or maybe 'preoccupied', suggesting that the combination of betting and watching sport is consuming so much of my attention that there is nothing left for the real people in my life. And thus I am losing touch with reality. And thus I am 'addicted'.

But I really have to say bollocks to all that.

Because I think it is coming from a bad place. A place where they are reluctant to acknowledge that a man can go to the swimming pool in Arklow with his ten-year-old daughter, followed by a movie in the newly opened Bridgewater Centre and then something to eat in Eddie Rockets, and have a nice time with her, the quality of which is unaffected by his checking out the result of the East Midlands derby on the car radio on the way home.

I can do all these things, I promise you.

Maybe it's a male thing, this ability to 'compartmentalize', as they say, but I doubt it. And who says it's a bad thing anyway?

Thanks to this facility, I can be experiencing a bitter defeat in a tennis match on the ATP website, and I can keep my head, when others might be losing theirs.

As a rule I do not involve my family in the pain or the joy of punting. I don't think that would be good for them, or for me.

I do not cry out in agony, or holler with delight. I only do that when I am watching Liverpool FC, which as I have explained is a different thing altogether, involving a different range of emotions. It would not feel right to be kicking the furniture in front of my ten-year-old daughter when Andy Murray loses me the money in a tiebreak in the fifth set, an outpouring of grief which, when I'm watching Liverpool, has become routine.

When there's money on it, I seem to be able to resist banging my head off the steering wheel and other such embarrassing methods of self-harm. Which again suggests that gambling, by its nature, is just not like a football match featuring your favourite team, or an open form of recreation such as a walk in the park.

It is something you generally keep to yourself. Which is probably another reason why it can go undiscovered as an addiction, until it is far too late.

And yet . . . I still feel that the use of pejorative words such as 'isolated' and 'detached' and 'preoccupied' is coming from a bad place. A place where the maleness of the activity is perhaps its most damning aspect, in the eyes of the accusers.

For example, let us imagine a form of low-level

escapism which, according to the stereotypical view, appeals mainly to females – the nightly soap operas, or popular fiction.

And let us imagine for a moment that I was to start speaking in ominous tones of how women with their immersion in these forms of low-level escapism are 'isolating' themselves. That they are using these things to avoid reality. That they are addicted to them. In a bad way.

If I ran that one up the flagpole, I would rightly be regarded as a sexist of the old school, a man who is taking the most pejorative view of these activities just because it suits his antediluvian worldview, a man who would deny these women their harmless recreations, their life-affirming amusements, their splendid isolation indeed, which is a fitting reward for their fine contributions in the home and in the workplace, their sterling service to humanity in general.

But am I just being defensive here?

Bearing in mind that 'defensive' is a word used in psychobabble as a means of attacking anyone who argues reasonably and rationally in his own favour, I will nevertheless attempt a frank assessment.

The answer is No.

And yet . . . and yet, the essential maleness of sports betting is a deeply interesting thing.

For me, as a boy, becoming a horse-player was one of the first truly independent things I did, using my own money, making my own decisions, even being brought into the company of men.

George Washington may have called it the child of

avarice, the brother of iniquity and the father of mischief, but gambling is also a road to freedom. Or at least that's how it looks on a good day. It promises a way of surviving entirely on your own wits, a way of making a living without actually working – yes, a road to freedom.

Even if, at some level, you always know that it is an illusory freedom, it's still an illusion that never seems to lose its appalling power.

I guess the Iron John crowd might see it as the boy venturing into the forest, accepting the challenge of forces greater than himself, testing himself in combat, but at a level that ensured he would always live to fight another day.

Yes, being a horse-player was 'isolating', with its intensity and single-mindedness, but it was isolating in a good way. It protected me from various beasts of the forest such as the beast of boredom, which Schopenhauer described as life's second-greatest burden (second only to survival), 'which hovers over every secure life like a bird of prey'.

It concentrated the mind. It gave me a hit of adrenalin of the type I couldn't get anywhere else, and which I felt was vital to the survival of my spirit and the preservation of my mental health.

And it taught me early doors that in life these pleasures do not come cheap.

I say that betting is not a communal activity, and yet there is a sense in which you feel connected to the sports betting community as a whole, which of course largely consists of other men. Perhaps we use our membership of this community to measure ourselves against other men, to validate our own masculinity, and again to pursue our damnable need to be proved right all the time.

It was not for nothing that Dostoevsky would have his gambler declaring, 'I had dared to run the risk! And now I was a man again!' For the mighty Russian, it was as simple as that: the punter who digs himself out of the hole restores his manhood.

Men have lost the pub, once an apparently inviolable fastness. They have lost the jobs that they were uniquely able to do, jobs that just don't exist any more. Yet the technology that made so many of them redundant now fills their days with sport. When they switch on that machine and commune with the mysteries of sports betting, they are at ease with themselves and with their fellow men, such a rare thing.

So, yes, the internet is a place where a man can feel free, albeit in a world which is not the real world – it is better than that.

14 April 2008

⚑   400 on Woods to win the Masters @ 11/10 – **Lose**

. . . –500

And so I am crushed.

I did the right thing, making the big investment in order to garner the maximum return, but it just didn't happen for me.

For four long and exhilarating and exhausting days at Augusta I watched Tiger inexorably climbing up the leaderboard, or at least staying where he was while everyone else slid down the leaderboard – and then there was just Immelman . . .

Is there any consolation in coming so close, in 'getting a run for your money'?

No, fuck that, you'll always get a run for your money with Tiger, but the loss of 400 and the 440 I would have won means a swing of 840 on the balance sheet. And you have to have your eye in to get that back in a hurry.

'It's Tiger's to lose,' a friend quipped, with Tiger trailing by six shots going in to the last round. He hardly sank a putt for four days and still he finished second. Yes, every tournament that Tiger plays is his to lose.

And this is one he lost.

He just missed a few putts on the back nine, which he would never normally miss, and, to his own apparent mystification, he lost.

And I lost.

Like Tiger I too had to watch those putts staying out of the hole, each one a dagger through the heart which, unlike Tiger,

I could not heal with the knowledge that I am still the world number one.

I just lost, and yes, America lost.

And my guy who arrived with the 100 dollars would have lost, big-time. But by now he would also have absorbed many of the lessons of his new world, not least the language of business and finance. And he would no doubt join with me in addressing the issue of the overall net deficit of 500 in the context of 'start-up costs'.

So we are posting these figures for the first quarter (or even the first third), reflecting a shortfall in revenues, in the context of results which have been at the lower end of expectations.

Early indicators were positive. A long-term strategy has been put in place, and successfully implemented in several key markets. But in the area of major capital expenditure, towards the end of the quarter we have encountered turbulence – headwinds, you might say – perhaps an indicator of an overall downturn.

A refinancing package has been arranged, and in spite of the damaging knock-on effects of the bear market, backers are looking at those highly impressive early yields. Confidence is returning. Going forward.

Analysts agree that the shortfall is at the modest end of the scale, and that an injection of capital should see a return to profitability in the near-to-medium term. Again, backers will be aware that we have had to absorb start-up costs which are always unpredictable.

Now we will have to absorb start-up-again costs.

A MOMENT OF SOBER REFLECTION
THE ESSENTIAL TRIVIALITY OF POLITICS

ON THE DAY that Brian Cowen became leader of Fianna Fáil and Taoiseach-elect he was pictured in the *Sunday Independent* standing at the counter of Paddy Power in Tullamore.

In his paw he held a bunch of 50-euro notes. We don't know if he was about to hand them over the counter, or if the money had come in the opposite direction. It being Grand National Day, probably it was not coming in the opposite direction.

It struck me that, apart from the incongruity of a clearly seasoned punter like Cowen having a serious bet on the Grand National, which many of us would not touch with a bargepole, this was the perfect image of modern Ireland, a nation of punters, now led by a punter, in a world of punters.

In fact if he hadn't made it this far, perhaps Cowen might have gone the way of his contemporary Ivan Yates, once a Fine Gael minister and tipped as a future Taoiseach, now the major-domo of Celtic Bookmakers.

Yes, old Ivan did the maths. He contemplated the possibility of running the country, and came to the painful conclusion that he needed to be in a better place, where the action is. Which is why he is now steadily building his chain of betting offices rather than wasting his time drafting another Dail speech, responding to the Budget.

Remembering that Blue Square menu in which

'politics' was just another game to be punted on, the bookie was again calling it right here, with Ivan realizing the essential triviality of so much that occurs in the shrunken universe of politics, and taking on the more serious challenges of this sporting life.

And I think of Cowen too as I try to come to terms with the sadness of Tiger losing at Augusta. In this anecdote, Cowen's colleague, the punter and Minister for Finance Charlie McCreevy, had given him a tip for a horse on which Cowen duly had a large bet. And when the horse was beaten by a short head, Cowen was naturally in low spirits on the journey home. But McCreevy put it like this: 'Brian, we haven't lost that money,' he said. 'We know where it is. And some day we'll go back there, and we'll get it.'

Fine words.

Words which convey the punter's attitude to money as a liquid thing, which is neither entirely your own nor entirely the bookie's, but always moving – often in the wrong direction, it must be said, but moving nonetheless.

Always moving.

25 April 2008

- (100 on Karlovic to beat some-guy-whose-name-I-can't-remember @ 2/9 – **Lose**)
- 130 on Haase to beat Chukin @ 2/5 – **Win**
- 100 on Verdasco to beat Lapentti @ 4/11 – **Win**
- 100 on Davydenko to beat Minar @ 2/5 – **Win**
- 100 on Cornet to beat Cirsteau @ 4/7 – **Win**
- 100 on Garbin to beat Mamic @ 2/5 – **Win**
- 100 on Savchuk to beat Ani @ 4/7 – **Lose**
- 100 on Serra to beat Cipolla @ 1/2 – **Win**
- 100 on Benesova to beat Ani @ 1/2 – **Win**
- 100 on Kolkaata to beat Bangalore @ 4/6 – **Win**
- 100 on Carter to beat Hawkins @ 4/6 – **Win**
- 100 on McGrane to win China Open @ 4/7 – **Win**
- 200 on Selby to beat King @ 1/6 – **Lose**
- 100 on Murray to beat Volandri @ 8/15 – **Win**
- 320 on Murphy to beat Harold @ 1/7 – **Win**
- 100 on Perry to beat Dott @ 4/9 – **Win**
- 145 on Maguire to beat Hamilton @ 2/7 – **Win**

. . . −200
Deposit: 100

How do I do it? Partly by not counting the first bet, because it was, after all, a tennis match; and to keep my spirits up I am allowing myself the little luxury of starting with a winner.

As the Scottish comedian Arnold Brown used to say, 'Why not?'

Well, the more censorious of you might roll out a number of 'why nots'.

You might point to the insidious nature of this thing, the way that I started off recording every transaction diligently, only to let my standards slip in this way in order to hide from the raw truth of the numbers.

You might point out that I am only fooling myself, and that this is a deeply immature way for an adult to be carrying on. And you might be right.

You will throw that word 'denial' at me, and in your self-satisfied way, again, you might be right.

And yet I am not fooling myself, or anyone else, in the sense that I am, after all, drawing attention to these . . . shall we say . . . these . . . nuances . . . these . . . peccadilloes.

They do not amount to much, in the overall scheme, and if you insist, you can add a few hundred more to the final reckoning after Valhalla. Yet it's interesting the way the punter feels this need to wriggle free from the tyranny of due diligence.

Partly it shows how this thing reduces us to infantilism, like a child losing a game and wanting the best-out-of-three.

But I suspect it also has a useful purpose in keeping up our morale, and as such it has a strategic dimension. We do not see ourselves as petty clerks, but as men of vision, expansive individuals trying to manage a going concern while the grey men are getting in our way, with their carping about a few stray shillings – what we would call 'sundries', a sort of natural wastage which will occur in any enterprise. Like a large round of drinks that you find yourself buying unexpectedly, an allowable expense, and perfectly understandable in the context of, say, a tennis match in which your guy retired injured while he was leading, or a game of cricket that gets shortened by bad weather – shit happens, but you don't have to bring it home and preserve it in a jar just to make yourself feel virtuous.

So having lost 100 ridiculously on the Croat, the dreaded Ivo Karlovic, I just forgot about it and immediately felt better about myself and about life in general, which was perhaps the crucial fillip I needed to forge ahead and back all those winners. All gamblers are prone to this form of amnesia – you could call it gamnesia.

The purpose of gambling is not necessarily to be counting your money, the purpose of gambling is gambling. And anything which facilitates this is to be warmly embraced. And on this occasion, a mild attack of gamnesia worked for me.

Having been disappointed in the area of blue-chip investments, I reverted to my bad old ways of betting on tennis and golf and cricket and snooker matches at the Crucible, and within days I had recouped most of the losses sustained on my behalf by Tiger Woods.

But I feel no guilt about this either – their money is just as good.

Yes, some Russian lady I'd never heard of called Benesova turned a decent profit for me, while the Tiger was lying low after the agonies of Augusta, having keyhole surgery on his knee. Meanwhile, his loyal backers were having a similar procedure done on the old Visa card.

Now, like the wise peasant with his careful husbandry, I have built up my resources again, relentlessly, in small increments, undeterred by the occasional setback.

Perhaps the average stake of 100 clears the mind somehow, giving me one less thing to think about on this quest.

So I am at that place where I have been twice before, roughly at the 500 mark in my current account, representing an acceptable overall deficit of 200. And twice before I have plummeted from that place into the dirt.

How do I do it?

Certainly I need to contemplate this matter deeply, because it seems that when I reach the magic half-grand mark, I am hitting some sort of a glass ceiling. I don't feel that I am doing things differently when I reach that mark, and yet I have been getting different results – losing results – after a sustained and even leisurely period of winning.

This time I will break through that glass ceiling. This time I will break on through to the other side. This time . . .

I don't believe that the punter has a quota of winners that he simply can't exceed, due to some law of averages known only to Paddy Power and William Hill. After all, the punter is not obliged to bet on everything, in fact he is not obliged to bet on anything at all, whereas the bookie is more or less obliged to take bets on everything – one of the few real advantages we have over them.

So I don't believe there is some mathematical inevitability to this, some cosmic rule whereby you can win a certain amount (in my case apparently 500) and then inevitably you start giving it all back.

Yet the bookies almost take it for granted that when a punter wins, as surely as night follows day, he will eventually give it all back, and then some – unless, of course, he is a she, who doesn't understand how it works, and who walks off with the money to do other things.

So I have been here before, looking through this glass ceiling.

Perhaps this brings into play some downtrodden aspect of the punter's character, some lack of entitlement on our part. Maybe we feel that we simply don't deserve to be winning at such an obviously immoral game. And subconsciously we are willing our own destruction.

Yet there are some punters who clearly don't see any glass

ceiling, or any ceiling made out of anything. The legendary ones have no limits, and then there are the everyday professionals who seem to feel that they are perfectly entitled to make a living at this thing of ours.

Time was, there were about three people in Ireland going around calling themselves professional gamblers. Now in these days of punting frenzy they seem to be everywhere. And perhaps they are privy to some wisdom that the rest of us lack, perhaps they just have the confidence which any professional has, which distinguishes him from the amateur.

Certainly you will see the odd interview with these men of mystery, in which their wisdom is sought. And it all sounds quite impressive, but on closer study it doesn't seem particularly wise to me. One genius, for example, describes how every day he prices up loads of events himself, and only then does he look at the bookies' prices. And if the bookies' prices are better, he feels a 'value' bet coming on.

We all do this to some extent, with each individual proposition, when we're trying to decide what to back. We may not sit down early in the morning with the old ready reckoner, but then maybe we don't feel the professional's need to make our punting feel like a proper day's work.

Still, he would look at my glass ceiling of 500 euros and know that he was made of different stuff.

Nor would he identify greatly with Dr Tom Dennehy of Bantry who won 240 grand recently on some mad accumulator that cost him 30 euros. Tully's of Bantry was the office which got stung, though the industry at large doesn't mind taking such a hit now and again, because like the Lotto winner with his huge cheque, the publicity is invaluable.

When the mug punter hears of a guy walking in with 30 euros and walking out with a quarter-million, he feels a surge of hope. It reminds him of his own finest hour, a bit like the 24-handicap hacker who tends to hit just the one magical golf shot by accident in an otherwise shocking round, but who is drawn back again and again by the thought of that one shot.

How did Dr Tom Dennehy do it? It involved twenty bets of €1.50 each on three golf tournaments including the Masters, and some godawful race on the all-weather.

Somehow from this morass the good doctor ended up collecting 240,000 euros. And not giving it back.

He told RTE he will probably buy a house in Cork.

9 May 2008

♏	50 on Deccan Chargers to beat Rajasthan Royals @ 4/7 – **Lose**
●	100 on Federer to beat Nalbandian @ 4/5 – **Win**
●	100 on Federer to beat Djokovic @ 10/11 – **Win**
—●	100 on O'Sullivan to beat Williams @ 2/7 – **Win**
⚐	100 on Darren Clarke to win Asia Open @ 4/5 – **Win**
—●	100 on Maguire to beat Perry @ 5/6 – **Lose**
⚽	270 on Man Utd to qualify against Barcelona @ 8/13 – **Win**
⚐	140 on Ochoa in three-ball @ 4/5– **Lose**
⚽	100 on Fiorentina to qualify against Rangers @ 2/5 – **Lose**
♏	100 on Kolkaata Knight Riders to beat Rajasthan Royals @ 5/6 – **Lose**
—●	300 on O'Sullivan to beat Hendry @ 1/3 – **Win**
⚐	70 on Clarke to beat Zanotti @ 1/2 – **Lose**
●	100 on Starace to beat Cilic @ 4/9 – **Win**
●	100 on Soderling to beat Korolev @ 4/11 – **Lose**
●	200 on Cañas to beat Naso @ 4/11 – **Win**
●	140 on Murray to beat Del Potro @ 4/9 – **Win**
●	100 on Robredo to beat Chela @ 2/5 – **Win**
♏	100 on Chennai Super Kings to beat Deccan Chargers @ Evens – **Lose**
♏	420 on Deccan Chargers to beat Chennai Super Kings @ 1/8 in-running – **Win**
●	100 on Blake to beat Seppi @ 6/5 – **Win**
●	100 on Blake to beat Verdasco @ 10/11 – **Win**
⚐	100 on Garcia to beat Choi @ Evens – **Win**

. . . +200

And so I break through that glass ceiling. Twice, in fact, I break through it.

The first time, unfortunately, I fell back through it, after a pivotal defeat for Stephen Maguire at the Crucible – ah, to think there was a time when millions of us would watch the World Snooker Championship for two weeks without betting, or even thinking of betting. How did we do it?

Maguire managed to lose 13–12 to Joe Perry, having recovered from an early 4–0 deficit, at which point I had pounced at the wondrous price of 5/6. But despite coming back strongly, Maguire later confessed that he was never quite focused on the game, that he underestimated Joe Perry, with whom he later reportedly joined in a late-night karaoke session.

So it seems that Maguire took his defeat better than I did. Because a win at that point would have sent me in the general direction of 1,000 in my account in this critical phase.

Alas, it was not to be.

Reflecting on Maguire's failure to get himself into the zone, I thought of that old AA line that 'expectations are just resentments under construction'. This line, when applied to the daily life of the punter, suggests that the punter with his great expectations is deep into the construction business, building resentments on a scale which would strike fear into the heart of McAlpine's Fusiliers.

And that's without the spectre of our old friend 'unusual betting patterns', mentioned yesterday in the illustrious context of a match between Accrington Stanley and Bury, which Bury won 2–0.

Even when the punter is receiving 100 per cent commitment on the field of play, he can experience feelings of intense hatred towards the golfer missing a ridiculously short putt, or the tennis player smashing a simple volley into the net, or retiring injured, or John Arne Riise scoring an own goal in the last second of injury time in the Champions League semi-final.

Though he knows that the perpetrator bears him no ill-will, and did not invite the punter to make the investment, still the punter is visited by these feelings of hatred, and by equally irrational feelings of love towards the ones who come through for him.

It all passes so quickly, of course – I've already forgiven Lorena Ochoa for letting me down last week, after all I've done for her – because hope always returns with each new day, each new programme of events on the screen, full of possibilities.

Hope and history rhyme in that poem by Seamus Heaney, though there's no escaping the fact that hope also rhymes with dope. Actually it rhymes a lot better with dope than it does with history.

But hey, we've got our own little bit of history here, as we march through the 800 barrier in the current phase, on the road to God-knows-where.

Thankfully we forget these resentments so quickly: James Blake cost me dearly at Wimbledon last year, yet I put all that aside to back him in Rome on his least favourite surface of clay, and, my word, the man delivered.

An emotional reunion this with Blakey, coming against the backdrop of some rather interesting punts, all winners – 300 on Ronnie O'Sullivan at the Crucible, 270 on Man Utd in the Champions League semi-final, and a most interesting 475 on the Deccan Chargers to beat the Chennai Super Kings in the Indian Premier League. Most interesting, because I also backed the Chennai Super Kings to beat the Deccan Chargers in the same match. But when it started to get away from the Super Kings, I took advantage of the 'in-running' facility, recovering roughly half my stake of 100 by investing 420 at 1/8.

I'm told that the 'shrewdies' are adept at managing their funds in this way, getting out when the time is right, clawing something back. I managed it here, and I guess the only down-side is that it leaves you slightly vulnerable to total devastation, and perhaps suicide. Because if, like me, you plunge on the very short odds as a 'saver', and in some sick way the baleful gods contrive to turn the game around, you are in an invidious position – not only have you lost a load of money plunging at 1/8 or even 1/16, chasing the free money, but you will also receive your winnings on the original, smaller bet, to remind you that you called it right in the first place. You just couldn't see it through, you didn't hold your nerve.

And that's tough.

You were right, and still somehow you fucked it up horribly. It is victory and defeat wrapped up in the same ugly package. It is victory with no reward, victory which may even leave you broke. And it is defeat without honour.

It happens.

It doesn't happen much, but it happens.

And when it happens, for the fallen punter the room with nothing in it except a chair, a table, a bottle of good whiskey and a loaded revolver must seem like the only acceptable option.

You hear these chilling tales of the guy who had £100,000 on Tottenham at 1/100 in an FA Cup match in which they were 3–0 up at half-time against Manchester City, who were reduced to ten men. City eventually won 4–3. So to win a grand, at half-time this guy had staked 100 grand, thinking that he wouldn't refuse a free thousand pounds if someone offered it to him in the street, so why should he refuse it now from the bookies? He never for a moment contemplated defeat, the odds against it were astronomical.

But it happened. And he had to watch it happening on live TV.

And it doesn't have to happen much to cover whatever losses the bookies might incur in providing this clawback facility to the shrewdies, offering me half my money back with only a very slight risk that I would be left with no option but to commit suicide.

Still, I love the Indian Premier League, live on Setanta every afternoon, though I'm finding it damnably hard to back a winner.

Through internet gambling I have discovered cricket, which brings me much joy. In particular it has started a love affair with India, whose star cricketers are keeping the very spark of civilization alive in the troubled subcontinent.

I watch Youvraj Singh or Sachin Tendulkar hitting a six with a magnificent strike celebrated by dancing girls, who are almost naked, shaking their booties to the pounding music, and I think of a few million Islamists up the road in Pakistan, maddened by the sight of these orgies of sport and money and sex and the lowest of the low, all that gambling.

Not only is the Indian Premier League a fine adornment to this sporting life. It is a road to freedom.

12 May 2008

⌐   35 on Harrington in three-ball @ 10/11 – **Lose**

⌐   100 on Ochoa in three-ball @ 11/10 – **Lose**

⌐   100 on Perry to beat Langer @ 4/5 – **Win**

⌐   100 on Mickelson to beat Langer @ 4/9 – **Lose**

⚽   800 on Man Utd to beat Wigan @ 1/4 – **Win**

. . . +250

A MOMENT OF SOBER REFLECTION
RISKING EVERYTHING AFTER ALL MY HARD WORK

WE MUST PAUSE here to mark this solemn occasion, the placing of a bet of 800 euros on a single event, in this case the deciding match of the 2007/2008 Premiership season between Man Utd and Wigan.

The bet was on Man Utd, of course, to win the match at odds of 1/4. Which they did, 2–0. So while the stake was approximately 400 more than my biggest bet so far, the odds were on the conservative side.

A fine balance there, between risk and reward.

I was risking everything here, looking at zero in my account after all my hard work. Yet I was confident enough in the outcome to justify that risk to myself, and to extract as much profit as I could on the day – a profit of 200, or 25 per cent, which, as I will never tire of saying, is considerably better than you'll be getting at the Bradford & Bingley.

Thus I have rededicated myself to the belief that this is the optimum business model for me to adopt, going forward. And I'm sure that my man trying to make his way in America would be thinking along these lines too, given that we're still in funds, and forging ahead, which is more than can be said for most.

By building up 'ammunition', I can use it to my advantage by plunging on what I regard as sure things. Rightly or wrongly. After all, there's no point in having the thick end of a grand in your account if you don't use it wisely. If you don't deploy it as a weapon, you should simply withdraw it to the sanctuary of your Visa card.

But I can tell you that there is a unique frisson to be had when you move into this strange new place where everything is on the line. You have an acute sense of how close you are to ruination, and yet you also feel you are taking on the enemy in the only way that can actually hurt him.

Again, the enemy here was offering many distractions. On this one match between Man Utd and Wigan, here are some of the markets that were available on Blue Square:

Draw No Bet, Total Goals, Total Goals Over/Under, Handicap, Double Chance, Half-time Result, Correct Score, Half Time/Full Time, Team To Score First, Time of First Goal, Total Goal Minutes, Half With Most Goals, Team Specials, Teams To Score, Winning Margins, Team Goals, Goalscorer Match Bet, Total Corners, Corners Match Bet, Total Bookings Points, Bookings Points Match Bet, Time Of First Card, First Team Carded, Red Cards, First Card, First Card Method, Player Specials, Player To Score, To Score A Hat-Trick, First Goalscorer, Last Goalscorer, Scorecast . . .

Clearly a man of my experience will be immune to all that mug punting . . . though I confess that at times in my life I have been so bored, I have entered the market on yellow cards . . . and OK, I went through a little phase when I wagered on the number of corner kicks . . .

> But I have put away such things, in favour of the supreme clarity that can only be found when I put my tank on one team to win the football match in 90 minutes. On the extremely rare occasions I experience that supreme clarity, as they say in the rooms of AA – in a slightly different context – I am in the right place.
>
> Some may have a more nuanced position, and may quibble with the exact choice of words here. For 'right' they would say 'wrong'.
>
> The wrong place.

20 May 2008

- 100 on Robredo to beat Kohlschreiber @ 8/11 – **Win**
- 100 on Tipsarevic to beat Montanes @ 13/8 – **Lose**
- 500 on Sharapova to beat Woznieki @ 2/9 – **Win**
- 100 on Clarke to beat Dredge @ 4/5 – **Lose**
- 100 on Tsonga to beat Montanes @ 1/4 – **Win**
- 100 on Calleri to beat Patience @ 2/7 – **Win**

. . . +300

Paddy Power says it expects to earn about £82 million in operating profit this year, up 14 per cent from 2007 and 9 per cent above the 'general consensus forecast'. In the first twenty weeks to 13 May, 'favourable sporting results' (our old friend) and 'top-line growth' have more than offset adverse foreign exchange movements, resulting in 'gross win ahead of expectations', chairman Fintan Drury said in a statement prior to the AGM.

Embittered punters will mutter that it's also a matter of volume, that the more betting there is, and the more things there are to bet on – many of them sponsored by betting corporations – overall the sporting results just can't help being favourable. That would also be their general consensus forecast, going forward.

They forget that Paddy Power too needs to get the breaks, that he too can have the bad days, when the top top players are knocking around.

'The outlook for Paddy Power remains strong,' said chairman Drury, reassuringly.

Ladbrokes weigh in with the news that the amount it has won from Irish punters was up 43 per cent in the first four months of the year.

And with all the major bookies, it hardly needs to be mentioned any more that a large percentage of their 'profitability' is coming from their online operations – generally it's gone past the halfway point, and it is going ever upwards.

It seems that everything is going down the toilet in this country except the one thing. Or as the Ladbrokes chief executive put it, 'whilst our business has seen no evidence yet of a consumer downturn, we remain mindful of general economic conditions'.

Indeed.

Mindful too that their high rollers seem to be mysteriously wiped out. Ladbrokes' profit from 'high rollers' during this period was £40 million. But the statement added that 'their activity had recently fallen to minimal levels'.

Since high rollers are unlikely to be radically changing their ways and investing in porkbelly futures to get them through these troubled times, one can only assume that they really have lost it all, that they have no money, or at least no money to bet with, which to them is the same thing.

In this challenging environment at least my own projections are on target, with 300 landing in my coffers from way back, as Portsmouth win the Cup. So the gods were not angry after all that I had factored in these profits, quietly confident that 160 on Portsmouth at 5/6 at the semi-final stage was free money.

So it has come to pass, though there is always something there to remind you of the fragile nature of this thing of ours.

I was watching Portsmouth winning in the TV room of a hotel, when a fellow sportsman left the room. And I couldn't help overhearing him, from the next room, making a call to his bookmaker, to have 50 each way on a horse at York.

Online bookies were offering odds on who would be the first player at Wembley to place the lid of the Cup on his head, and this man was still backing horses, no doubt figuring that he was the sensible fellow. What had he to hide, that he couldn't have made that bet without leaving the room and lowering his voice to no practical effect?

I guess there is still some shame attached to these things, and perhaps rightly so. I checked later, and his horse finished nowhere.

Another 'favourable sporting result' there. And for all we know, even a bit of 'top-line growth'.

22 May 2008

♔ 100 on Kings XI Punjab to beat Mumbai Indians @ 2/5 – **Win**

⚽ 140 on Man Utd to win Champions League Final @ 8/11 – **Win**

. . . +440

Withdraw: 500

Another solemn moment here, as I smash through the 1,000 barrier. Not 1,000 overall, but 1,000 in my account at present, which was once 100 successfully deposited after the tragedy of Augusta.

So in the last month I have made roughly a grand, representing a profit of approximately 1,000 per cent, which you could hardly hope to get from the Bradford & Bingley even with the aid of a sawn-off shotgun. This will go a long way towards wiping the slate clean before the next phase of the quest, which now beckons.

Inspired by this breakthrough, I will indeed make my first successful withdrawal. I will withdraw 500, leaving me with an overall running profit of 440, which is not bad, not bad at all.

And it is done. 'Withdraw Successful', it says. And as the money moves instantly from my Blue Square account to my Visa account, I can sense the howls of anguish all the way from Alderney.

Yes, it is permitted to press the Withdraw button as well. To take as well as to give. Which creates this strange sensation in the punter that he has briefly been seized by the spirit of Woman.

The reason why bookies fear women, and hate them, is that apart from the rare ones who are addicted they tend to have an unnatural fondness for that Withdraw button.

Not that women are immune to the pleasures of predicting the future. There is a vast and frankly disgraceful global industry of fortune tellers and mystics who, for a small fee, will reveal to a largely female clientele what's going to happen for the rest of their lives.

Men don't subscribe to this foolishness. They don't care about who they're going to marry or when they're going to die, they just want a few winners. And if they get it right, they make sure they get paid for it.

And then they make sure that they give it all back.

Indeed, bearing in mind the famous old battle cry of the *Guardian*'s racing correspondent Richard Baerlein that 'now is the time to bet like men', the original working title of this diary was 'Betting Like Men, Winning Like Women'.

And if not exactly winning – not yet – by leaving 440 in my account as a fighting fund, I am at least wiping out the losses inflicted on me early doors by the likes of Tiger Woods.

But as I even up the score, it is also a time to remember my fallen comrades. Because the two victories above were achieved by the thinnest possible margins – a penalty shoot-out in Moscow, and one run in India. Just the one.

Many of my comrades would have been on the wrong end of these margins, and my thoughts are with them today.

It was probably easier to stay alive on Omaha beach than to stay ahead at this game, in which death can call at any time, in a thousand ways. A few millimetres either way, and instead of crossing the 1,000 line I'd be sinking back towards 500.

Indeed I was damn near wiped out during these exchanges, due to a rush of blood which almost persuaded me to put everything on the Mumbai Indians 'in-running', when it looked like the game was getting away completely from the Kings XI Punjab.

One run . . . if I'd gone with that rush of blood, that one run would have cost me a grand in the most ignominious way.

And no doubt it ended up costing other men a grand, and a lot more besides.

But I must pay tribute to myself for my fortitude at that defining moment, and for my thoroughness in the Champions League. I came down on the side of United only after making a call to my friend John Giles, probably the world's leading authority on the subject. John favoured United slightly, but advised a modest investment. And that was good enough for me.

And so I approach the French Open tennis in roaring fettle, armed with plenty of ammunition and the latest report from an independent panel which has revealed that forty-five tennis matches over the last five years remain under suspicion because of 'unusual betting patterns'.

The panel is at pains to state that 'professional tennis is neither systematically nor institutionally corrupt', but then with all those games under suspicion, it wouldn't have to be, would it?

'We have found no evidence of any Mafia involvement in corrupting tennis,' the review declares. And then it adds: 'We do not doubt that criminal elements may be involved in seeking to subvert or corrupt some players or officials and that they may even involve organized criminal gangs.'

Indeed.

So it's not the mafia, it's just organized criminal gangs.

25 May 2008 – Roland Garros starts today

There was a time when the French Open tennis championship meant nothing to me.

But internet betting has turned that around, to the extent that I now regard Roland Garros, and Wimbledon which follows next month, as my busy time.

But while it might be my busy time as a punter, as a sportsman I have yet to be captivated by tennis in the way I have been captivated by the great game of cricket.

They are not my people, the ones you hear laughing heartily when a pigeon flies across Centre Court, interrupting the match. They are not my people, the lawyers and the diplomats you see lounging around Roland Garros, and as for Sue Barker and the folks who gather each year on Henman Hill – no, they are not my people.

In fact the Russian investors who love tennis because there are no draws are probably more my people than the brigadiers of the All-England Club.

There is still something unacceptably twee about the world of tennis, a sense that it's the sporting equivalent of those fake easy-listening classical music records, which are music for people who don't really like music – likewise, tennis is sport for people who don't really like sport.

And yet as a betting man my heart beats a little faster when I go to the Roland Garros website and I find Slamtracker, a truly superb thing whereby you can 'watch' every point of every game being played on the same page.

No punter could fail to be moved by this Slamtracker. It is a step beyond even the excellent ATP scoreboard, and it is also rolled out (in the appropriate livery of green and blue respectively) for Wimbledon and the US Open.

It is one of the most beautiful things I have ever seen.

8 June 2008

● 250 on Cañas to beat Odesnik @ 1/4 – **Lose**

● 220 on Robredo to beat Coria in-running @ 1/4 – **Win**

ⅲ 100 on Chennai Super Kings to beat Deccan Chargers @ 4/6 – **Win**

● 375 on Shiavone to beat Craybas @ 1/6 – **Win**

● 440 on Sharapova to beat Rodina in-running @ 1/3 – **Win**

● 100 on Szavay to beat Lisicki @ 1/3 – **Win**

● 100 on Benesova to beat Cetkovska @ 2/5 – **Lose**

● 100 on S. Williams to beat Srebotnik @ 4/9 in-running – **Lose**

● 140 on Murray to beat Almagro @ 11/8 – **Lose**

● 200 on Mathieu to beat Schwank @ 8/13 – **Win**

● 225 on Wawrinka to beat Gonzalez @ 8/15 – **Lose**

● 400 on Karlsson to beat Velasco @ 4/6 – **Lose**

— 125 on Atlanta to beat Cincinnati @ 4/5 – **Lose**

⌐ 100 on Donald in three-ball @ 1/2 – **Lose**

● 200 on Jankovic to beat Radwanska @ 2/5 – **Win**

⌐ 180 on Mickelson to beat Perez @ 8/13 – **Win**

— 100 on Oakland to beat Texas @ 4/5 – **Win**

● 100 on Dementieva to beat Zvonereva @ 4/6 – **Win**

● 200 on Sharapova to beat Safina @ 5/6 – **Lose**

● 330 on Monfils to beat Ljubicic @ 5/6 – **Win**

— 120 on NY Yankees to beat Minnesota Twins @ 4/7 – **Lose**

● 300 on Jankovic to beat Navarro @ 2/9 – **Win**

● 200 on Safina to beat Dementieva @ 4/7 – **Win**

● 180 on Kuznetsova to beat Safina @ 4/7 – **Lose**

●— 170 on Painter to beat Eccles @ 4/7 – **Win**

— 150 on Boston Red Sox to beat Tampa Bay Rays @ 4/5 – **Win**

⌐ 120 on Sorenstam in three-ball @ 4/6 – **Win**

● 110 on Ivanovic to beat Safina @ 4/11 – **Win**

Free Money

- ⚑ 270 on Ochoa to win McDonald's Championship @ 4/9 – **Lose**
- ⚑ 400 on Milkha Singh to win Austrian Open @ 1/5 in-running – **Win**
- ⚽ 480 on Dublin to beat Louth @ 1/8 – **Win**
- ⛰ 10 on Tartan Bearer to win The Derby @ 6/1 – **Lose**

. . . Even

After riding the roller coaster that is Roland Garros, and a few other roller coasters along the way, my profit in the overall context of the quest has been reduced from approximately 440 to approximately zero.

Which, from a certain perspective, means that I have lost about 440 in the last few days. Which, at first glance, might seem like a bad thing. But on closer examination it is actually a good thing, when you consider how much I might have lost.

Clearly the baleful gods were maddened by that successful withdrawal, and immediately began conspiring to claw it back, and a bit more besides.

First, I got the fever – an actual fever, a sickness that almost certainly clouded my judgement for at least seventy-two hours. And it was perhaps heightened by the Dostoevskan fever that grips the soul of the punter when he is forging ahead – 'gamblers know how a man can sit in the same place for nearly twenty-four hours, playing cards and never turning his eyes to the right or the left . . . ' that great Russian punter wrote.

Fever . . . it might well account for that loss on Andy Murray, who is clearly going to the bad and still swallowing up the money of loyal supporters such as myself. As he capitulated in Paris, I felt a sense of personal betrayal.

Lorena Ochoa too has been a grave disappointment to me.

Ah, but the margins are so excruciatingly thin. Last week I

marvelled at my good fortune in winning bets by one run, and one penalty kick. Now the gods were taking it all back, in like manner – Ochoa lost by one shot, as did Robert Karlsson in the most expensive defeat of them all, a loss of 400, when he somehow failed to beat some fellow called Velasco over eighteen holes.

The following day Karlsson threatened to break the course record while Velasco tumbled down the leaderboard, but I was left to dig myself out of the hole he had created for me. Which I did, somehow.

In fact in one terrible day I took a hit of 600, a combination of Karlsson's disappointing display and the inability of one Stanislas Wawrinka to beat Fernando Gonzalez at tennis, even though Wawrinka won the first two sets, a position from which I myself would not expect to lose. But lose he did.

So while the fever was running through me, making me mad, I found my fine profit destroyed, at which point, with Lady Luck cackling unmercifully, I was forced to deposit the 500 I had so successfully withdrawn, and which in turn was almost immediately devoured by my good friends in Alderney, as the situation worsened on all fronts.

Now I was 500 down overall, not for the first time.

What could I do but deposit another 200 to keep me going? What can any of us do in these circumstances? We get knocked down, and we get up again.

In this case, we get up to break-even again, making gains of 500 on that melancholy deposit of 200 – a 200 which we then withdrew, just to show those bastards that we haven't forgotten where the button is.

In fact the successful deposits and the equally successful withdrawals were coming so feverishly, for a moment I even thought I might have a wee problem with this gambling thing.

And did I say the margins are excruciatingly thin? Did I allude to that in any way? Obviously I don't like to dwell on these things, because that way lies total madness, but how about this: one shot either way in the Karlsson and Ochoa matches, and a win for Sharapova over Safina when she was a set and 5–2 ahead, and 5–2 ahead in the tiebreak, for Christ's sake, and I would now have about 1,500 more in the tank.

Which would be nice.

Then again, how about this: with the gun to my head, way down deep in the hole, I studied the market on Ljubicic v Monfils at Roland Garros, desperately needing to find the right answer.

And eventually I found it, by this process of reasoning: Ljubicic is a fine player and an admirable fellow, perhaps not the man he was, but a solid citizen, a fiercely competitive Croat who will always give you a run. Monfils, by contrast, is capable of anything. He is capable of winning from any position, however apparently hopeless, and he is also capable of losing from any position, however apparently unassailable. Therefore, if you're down to your last 330 euros, the choice is clear: you put it all on Monfils.

And of course he wins. Quite easily, in the end. Most impressively, in fact.

There is undoubtedly something about that last throw of the dice which can inspire the punter to leave his reason behind, and to engage with more volatile forces.

If indeed I had been 1,500 ahead, I would not have wasted even 10 of it on Gael Monfils – as you may have noticed, I had a 'housewife's bet' of a tenner on Tartan Bearer in the Derby (*quelle surprise*, he finished second). All things being equal, I would actually prefer to waste that tenner on a horse than to waste it on the likes of Gael Monfils. But when all things are not equal ... when we are down and troubled, it is then that we engage with forces beyond our ken, because we are getting no response from the forces within our ken. It is then that we ask the question, and to our own amazement we get the answer: Gael Monfils.

And it is the right answer.

My fortunes restored, I decide to reward myself with a free bet. Hell, these corporate fucks are always giving themselves little bonuses for performances which are far less uplifting, in fact for no good reason at all.

So I have 300 on Djokovic at 13/2 to win the French Open. Partly the free bet is to compensate me for the damage done to me by the fever. And in keeping with this generosity of spirit, it is a wildly optimistic punt on Djoko, who duly gets annihilated by Nadal in the semi-final. But even without a sicknote we always enjoy a free bet – even if this is the sort of free bet that we're paying for with our own money.

So after all these vicissitudes, I am still (approximately) keeping to the Warren Buffett standard – first, do not lose money. And I think again of my man trying to make his fortune in the New World, who would by now be getting a visceral sense of how hard it is, how the struggle never gets any easier, how elusive the big prizes can be.

But he, like me, may reflect on the fact that being a few quid in profit puts us about a million ahead of a top Premiership star and England international who is reported today to have massive gambling debts – there are several strong contenders, but I know who my money is on.

One's deepest sympathies are also extended to Michael O'Leary of Ryanair, who last year decided against hedging the price of Ryanair's oil supplies, a decision which turned out to be considerably more expensive than the combined total of all the beaten dockets I have held since 1972 or thereabouts . . . and I've held a few.

Nor do we take any pleasure in the official confirmation that world stock markets lost $5.2 trillion in January. Though when you recall that Jérôme Kerviel lost five billion all by himself you get a sense of the market's endless possibilities.

So we are four-square behind the accountancy firm Mazar's, who tell us to 'treat cash as if it were gold dust'.

Yes, we will do that.

And in the light of our old refrain about getting a better return from your punting than you'll get from the Bradford & Bingley, we were saddened to learn today that a leading British bank has posted a severe profit warning, and that this bank was in fact . . . the Bradford & Bingley.

Nor did it escape our attention that in this uncertain climate for investors, there are radio ads on *Morning Ireland* for spread betting. They are offering 'tutorials' in spread betting, with a little low-key note at the end that this is 'a leveraged product in which you can lose more than your original investment'.

So we have the guy from Betfair who saw the Republic of Ireland manager market as an educational tool, and now we have 'tutorials' in spread betting. These 'tutorials' bring betting to its highest ever point of respectability, making it sound like an academic discipline, something akin to medieval history – with that slight understated difference that 'you can lose more than your original investment'.

It's like studying the career of Charlemagne and the rise of the Carolingian Empire. Except you can also lose your house.

Otherwise it's just the same.

16 June 2008

●   300 on Hewitt to beat Goodall in two sets @ 1/7 – **Win**

⚽   75 on France to win Euro 2008 @ 8/1 – **Unsettled**

♏   500 on India to beat Pakistan @ 1/6 in-running – **Win**

●   85 on Haas to beat Stepanek @ 1/3 in-running – **Win**

       (quick money – 30 in 30 seconds)

●   85 on Berdych to beat Soderling @ 4/6 – **Lose**

⚽   330 on Portugal to win Group @ 4/7 – **Win**

⚽   180 on Spain to win Group @ 2/7 – **Win**

⚑   100 on Garcia to beat Harrington in US Open @ 10/11 – **Win**

⚑   100 on Woods to win US Open @ 4/1 – **Unsettled**

... +340

And so the winners come, like rain on the parched earth.

But today I am engaged again with higher things, as I contemplate the prospect of this afternoon's eighteen-hole play-off for the US Open at Torrey Pines, between Rocco Mediate and my man Tiger Woods.

This is the 'Unsettled' bet, the one that I am waiting for, the one that all international sportsmen are waiting for, the one that America and the world is waiting for. Because later today we will not only find out if Woods can win his fourteenth Major in all, we will also find out if he can win his first Major using only one leg.

At Torrey Pines his right leg has been functioning normally, but his left leg is in a terrible state, as he recuperates from the operation on his knee that was performed immediately after the Masters back in April.

Readers will notice a certain symmetry, even a certain beauty,

149

in the fact that Tiger cost me 400 on that occasion, which is exactly what I would win today if he manages to bring it all back home using only one leg.

He has already come through things in the last four days that have filled the heart with terror and pity, but also with a sense of awe at his deranged magnificence. Many times at Torrey Pines he has taken out the big stick and walloped the ball 330 yards down the track, and been struck by a bolt of agony which for a few moments makes this most advanced creature in the history of the species look like a very old man, bent over his club in deep distress. But then using that club as a cane he has summoned up the courage to walk after that ball, and find it, and hit it again.

That he has made it through seventy-two holes with all this, and a hundred euros of mine on his back, is, as we say in the mortal realm, beyond belief. And there are those who *genuinely* don't believe it, including a friend of mine, himself a fine amateur golfer, who became convinced at a certain point on the Saturday that Tiger's ball must be connected to a satellite system which somehow steered it 60 foot down the green and into the thirteenth hole for an eagle. An eagle which was needed at the time, because on this brutally hard track Tiger acquired an extra handicap, racking up a double-bogey six on the first hole, three days out of four.

Just to get his heart started.

So he needed another eagle too, on the thirteenth on the Saturday. And he got it, as the TV cameras showed the crowds rising in slow motion, wild with anticipation, and then going completely berserk as Tiger nailed another one.

And in the end he needed a birdie on the same eighteenth hole yesterday, with a horrible 12-foot putt that no other man on earth would have sunk in that situation. Even with the assistance of the latest satellite technology.

One shot, and not two, to keep it going until the next day, to play another eighteen holes, making it ninety altogether, using only the one leg. One shot, after a bad drive down the eighteenth into a bunker, and a poor second shot into the primary rough. And then a magical wedge dug out of the long grass to give him a chance. One shot, or the last four days of suffering would all be in vain.

Lee Westwood too had a chance, on the last green, a 20-foot downhill putt. Which he missed.

One shot.

But Westwood needed two. He had witnessed at close quarters one of those odd moments of humanity from Tiger on the thirteenth, when Westwood hooked his ball into the hazard, and then Tiger, eschewing the safe iron shot and the lay-up which would have brought him an important par, decided inexplicably to have a crack at the green, which landed in the same hazard as Westwood.

But then Tiger screws things up just like anyone else, because to err is human, and if we did not know for sure that he was human, we would not rightly connect with the miracles.

So how did this man become available at odds of 4/1 to win the tournament? Evidently my good friends in Alderney formed the view that when Tiger double-bogeyed the first hole on the first day, and then threw in a bogey, while he appeared to be struggling with a career-threatening injury, it was safe enough to allow him to drift out to 4/1 while he was still play-ing the front nine on the Thursday.

Maybe it wasn't too crazy to let him drift, because, after all, he doesn't win them all. He didn't win that seven-in-a-row at the WGC, he didn't win the Masters, did he?

But I formed a different view. I believe that if Tiger Woods is available at 4/1 to win anything, in any context or in any condition, you are almost morally obliged to take those odds. In fact if Tiger Woods were available at 4/1 to become the leading goalscorer at the Euro 2008 football tournament, I might not go in there with all guns blazing, but I'd certainly think about it.

As I write, in southern California it is six in the morning and he is probably waking up, having a few swing-thoughts to get him into a good place mentally for the play-off against Rocco Mediate, which starts at nine.

'Mr Woods, Mr Woods, Mr Woods are you insane? Are you out of your mind?' Rocco had exclaimed after the third round, humbled by what he'd seen.

And Rocco knows as well as anyone that when they tee it up today the contest is between Mr Woods' mind and Mr Woods' body, with Rocco as a sort of playing spectator awaiting the outcome.

As I write, in the mind's eye Mr Woods is being helped out of bed by a team of ashen-faced medics, and they're telling him that overnight they've been looking at the X-rays of his poor destroyed knee, and if he goes golfing they can't be responsible for what happens out there.

Tiger hears what they're saying at one level, but at another level he can't hear a thing.

He just wants to win.

⌐ 100 on Tiger Woods to win US Open @ 4/1 – **Win**

17 June . . . +740

As our Islamic friends might say: 'It was written.'

A Bit of Previous
EURO 2008 AND THE PERFECT ADDICTION STORM

EURO 2008 is on at the moment. Like the 'shrewdies', I figure that Spain must have a big chance, but too many of us have lost too much money over the years on Johnny Spaniard to go there again. He is the football equivalent of Harchibald, the Noel Meade-trained hurdler who seems to have all the talent to be the Champion Hurdler for the foreseeable future, yet who just doesn't seem to know how to win – or when to win. And who has been the downfall of many a good man.

But as we prepare to submerge ourselves in another of these great sporting festivals which bring such joy to our lives, this may be the right time – if there ever is a right time for these things – to tell the addiction therapist that there is one addiction I haven't mentioned yet.

I know that this is deeply frustrating for the addiction professional, who has already had to listen to my excellent arguments which challenge the very essence of his or her worldview, but frankly, I believe I have a certain expertise in these areas too. The expertise of the practitioner.

So while I would question the blunt assertion from certain quarters that I am 'an alcoholic', and while I am demonstrating daily that I am addicted to gambling only up to a point, I'd have to accept that I am almost certainly addicted, in a meaningful way, to television. Without all that sport on TV, I don't believe that my internet gambling would be nearly as enjoyable. And I'm sure the same goes for my brethren in the global fellowship of punters.

And since a large percentage of the world's population is genuinely addicted to TV – it would be known in the trade as their 'primary' addiction – it seems that here lies the real genius of the global internet gambling phenomenon. They have taken one of the world's most common addictions – the addiction to TV – and onto it they have grafted all these other layers of addiction – the addiction to sport, the addiction to gambling, the addiction to the internet – to create the perfect addiction storm. They have made this fusion between the most ancient recreation of men and the most modern, and it works beautifully.

And if it is any consolation to the therapist, I can easily trace my own addiction to TV back to childhood – which is how they like it.

Always at this time of year I remember those summers spent in Blackrock, County Louth, which, being on the north-east coast, had one thing in particular that you couldn't get in the midlands, or in most other parts of Ireland at that time – it had the BBC. And ITV. And what the BBC and ITV were doing back then as a matter of routine is now regarded so highly that it is seen as the Golden Age of television.

From early in the morning till late at night, I devoured it. I gorged on it with the feverish hunger of a boy who was deprived of these wonderful things, who had to stuff it all in during the summer, as if that would keep me going for the rest of the year. Glued to *The Big Match* and *Grandstand*, with the curtains drawn against the bright August sunshine.

So in a strange way, this addiction – if you want to call it that – came about as much through enforced abstinence as through indulgence in these pleasures. If I had grown up in a better place which had the BBC and ITV, perhaps I would have had a normal relationship with television, instead of this quasi-bulimic regime of either starvation or gluttony, and nothing in between.

But it was so good . . . *Dad's Army, Fawlty Towers,* Eric and Ernie, *Sportsnight with (and without) Coleman, New Faces, This Is Your Life, Parkinson* . . .

When I first saw colour television, regardless of what it was showing at the time, I felt a bit like Howard Carter gazing into the tomb of Tutankhamun. But I devoured the sport with a par-ticular relish, and to this day when I am looking at the British Open, or the World Cup, or Royal Ascot, or the Olympics, or even Wimbledon for all its middle-class screeching, I am young again, and I will never grow old.

So Euro 2008 is on at the moment, and I am back in that place, except now I can switch on my console and enjoy this special Euro presentation which Blue Square has mounted with flags and emblems and all sorts of colourful extras, a bit like those rare occasions in days of yore when the racing pages would print the jockey's colours beside the name of the horse on Derby Day – ah, they must think that we are simple folk, who can be seduced by a bit of colour.

Simple folk who will be gambling 350 million quid on Euro 2008 in Britain alone, and this without England or Scotland or Wales or Ireland playing.

But perhaps the deepest peace of all settles with me, in the TV summertime, watching them teeing it up at the Open for four days on the BBC, uninterrupted by ads, at Troon or Royal Birkdale or Royal Lytham & St Anne's. I fear what might have become of me had the BBC in the late 1970s had the interactive facilities of today, such as Skybet. Back then I had no red button which I could press to start betting. I could not press that button to be offered the latest prices on whether John McEnroe would break his racket over the head of Vitas Gerulaitis, or whether some star of Zambia at the World Cup would get a red card because he's already on a yellow and by the look of him he's clearly extremely agitated about something.

The absence of that red button served as a sort of a prophylactic to any young man wanting to take it a step further. The sport in itself was deemed to be exciting enough, without giving you the extra options by which you could deepen the experience. But my equivalent today has that red button which permits him to enter a multitude of markets, a device which at all times places him in a situation of grave peril.

And as a result, he has almost no chance of turning out as well as I have.

21 June 2008

⚽ 75 on France to win Euro 2008 @ 7/1 – **Lose**

🐎 40 on Henry The Navigator @ 4/7 – **Win**

Ⅲ 20 on Durham to beat Lancashire @ 4/5 – **Win**

🎾 75 on Cañas to beat Bopanna @ 4/11 – **Win**

🎾 80 on Ljubicic to beat Troicki @ 1/4 – **Lose**

🐎 20 on Bankable @ 13/8 – **Lose**

⚽ 80 on Spain and Greece to draw @ 8/11 – **Lose**

⚽ 100 on Bolivia v Paraguay (time of next goal) @ 10/11 – **Lose**

🐎 10 on The Whole Sister @ 4/5 – **Lose**

Ⅲ 100 on Durham to beat Lancashire @ 8/11 – **Win**

Ⅲ 130 on Somerset to beat Worcestershire @ 8/11 – **Win**

⚽ 180 on Portugal to beat Germany @ 8/11 – **Lose**

🎾 90 on Kraijcek to beat Tanasugarn @ 4/9 – **Lose**

⛳ 100 on Ochoa to win Wegmans tournament @ 3/1 – **Lose**

⛳ 200 on Ochoa to win Wegmans tournament @ 6/5 – **Lose**

⛳ 25 on Goosen to win BMW tournament @ 5/2 in-running – **Lose**

⚽ 500 on Croatia to qualify against Turkey @ 2/5 – **Lose**

. . . –500

I am crushed. Again, in the most cruel and degrading fashion,
I am crushed.

What gets into us, that we'd be looking at Bolivia v Paraguay
on Sky Sports, and we'd find ourselves betting on the time of
the next goal?

What gets into us at all?

I'm sure there will eventually be some way to measure these
things scientifically, these quirks of brain chemistry, these
feelings of over-confidence after you've had a few winners and

you just can't envisage losing, even on Bolivia v Paraguay, and the time of the next goal.

Perhaps we are especially vulnerable to these feelings in the aftermath of a Tiger Woods victory, because we forget that everyone else lives in the mortal realm, where shit happens – and in the realm of South American football, for the punter, what else is there but shit?

But ultimately I am undone, not entirely by my own foolishness but by events which perhaps provide objective proof of the existence of Evil. Half of Europe indeed was undone in this way, because half of Europe apparently has been backing Croatia at Euro 2008, either to win the tournament or to win individual matches.

So when they lost to Turkey in a penalty shoot-out, after scoring the 'winner' in the last minute of extra-time only for the facking Turks to equalize somehow, with the last kick, it was one of these terrible events which connect us to something bigger than ourselves, to a world of suffering.

It helps to explain why organized criminals are reluctant to leave anything to chance, because chance is a fine thing but there's too much of it out there, and in extreme cases it can kill you.

Yes, you can see why they would prefer to pay a straight bribe to some player who might appreciate it, rather than relying on abstractions such as judgement and luck.

And you understand that so many betting 'strokes' are simply sporting frauds perpetuated by men who know the outcome in advance, inasmuch as anything can be known in this world.

Not that they are alone in their desire to minimize risk. Even in fields as apparently exalted as literature itself, in the most respectable publications you will see books being reviewed by friends or associates of the author, and understandably so – the risk that a novel which has taken ten years to write might fall into the hands of some dingbat reviewer and be destroyed is a risk that some of the more influential writers and their friends just refuse to contemplate.

And there is more than a grain of truth in the line that every great fortune was founded on a great crime – at a time like this, it really seems that the only way you can win the game is by rigging it. Certainly if you're relying on the kindness of the gods you are always exposed to unhappy endings.

Unhappy, and expensive too. Keen observers will already have noted that I had a 'monkey' (500) on the Croats, and I daresay that a lot of other men had a lot of monkeys out there that never came home.

Croat coach Slaven Bilic was reported to be 'philosophical'. And then he was quoted as saying that 'the pain of that defeat will stay with me for a long time. It will haunt us for ever.'

Yes, a few hundred thousand punters all across the continent were 'philosophical' too, if 'philosophical' means that the pain will stay with them for a long time and they will be haunted for ever. And for some of them, at least, it will be unbearable.

Since the turn of the century I have been writing about the growth of gambling, and from the start it has seemed clear to me that men who lose a lot of money gambling are more vulnerable than most to acts of self-destruction. By its nature, in many cases we can have no way of knowing exactly what pushes people over the edge, but even the 'experts' seem to understand that gambling is more likely than any other addiction to lead to suicide.

And it's not just a natural consequence of the fact that the majority of suicides are male, as are the majority of sports betters.

It's because the gambler tends to keep going until the very

end. So when he reaches the end, when he really can't get any more money from anywhere, it really is . . . the end.

And if by chance he reaches that place, by way of Croatia v Turkey in the quarter-final of Euro 2008, we can see how he might be driven to that final act of self-loathing.

If this indeed was the event on which the gambler went down big, and went down for the last time, it isn't too hard to imagine the gambler in question deciding that enough is enough, in every sense.

With its almost uniquely nightmarish ending, it represents not just a brutal defeat, but one which suggests to the victim that the forces ranged against him are just too great, that he is doomed in some special way, that he is just too unlucky to live.

The man in this situation would feel a terrible rage against the world, but also he would feel a terrible rage against himself. And while he is clearly powerless to destroy the world, there are all sorts of ways in which he can destroy himself.

And so it goes.

And what about my man in America?

In the light of these hellish events, I fear there is no future for him in this luckless new world. I fear it is time for him to get out now, before he finds himself in a situation from which he can never get out, a place of fools and madmen.

He is down, but when you look at it a certain way, he is still alive. So he can recover in a material sense, in time, and if he removes himself from this bad place, pretty soon he will probably get over the deep desire to kill himself.

But this morning many thousands of us know exactly how he feels. We know that this is not really about the loss of money, it is about the loss of our souls. So it is time to take a decision, to act responsibly. It is time for that man to walk away from it, to turn round and go home.

Frankly, I don't think he will need much persuading.

He must quit now, and go back to a better place, to the old country.

I will continue, because I have a higher commitment. But my advice to anyone on the wrong end of that Croatia defeat would be to stop. You don't need the baleful gods fucking with you in this way. Get out now, while you can. And don't look back.

Even if you still have the tiniest sliver of hope left in your being, don't look back.

Because remember, hope rhymes with history if you're Seamus Heaney, but if you're a punter watching the Turks equalizing with the last kick, hope doesn't rhyme with history.

Hope rhymes with dope, baby!

Hope rhymes with dope . . . and yet . . . and yet many of my punting instincts have been sound. I have backed many winners, but I felt I was entitled to a bigger return which can only come with the occasional monkey, wisely deployed.

And this was not an unwise monkey; in fact Croatia were celebrating their 'win' in the 119th minute, as indeed were we all.

And then, still high on the improbability of it all, we found ourselves pole-axed.

Fools will say that the bookie always wins, due to some mathematical formula which I have never understood, and which I assume to be bullshit. In fact a bookie told me last week that 'if the punter has enough ammunition, he'll get you in the end'.

Yet in the course of this journal, we are perhaps arriving at a deeper understanding of the inevitability of the punter's doom. It's not a mathematical thing, yet it has a profound sense of inevitability.

Free Money

We do not rightly understand why the sun rises every morning, we only know that it does, every time. Likewise, we don't understand why our biggest bets, our bravest bursts for freedom, invariably go down. We only know that they do.

One thinks again of the socialist Heywood Broun's mordant line that 'the urge to gamble is so universal, and its practice so pleasurable, that I assume it must be evil', and we wonder if the essential darkness of the activity means that good men, even the wisest of good men, just can't prosper at this game. Once again, 'it is written'.

And bad men can't prosper at it either.

*

So I am 500 behind again.

I am 500 behind with Wimbledon starting next week, accompanied by front-page headlines in *The Times* about match-fixing which are no surprise to me, but which may further complicate my journey to freedom.

Big bets went down too in the last few days on Lorena Ochoa, another carefully nurtured investment for which I can't really hate myself – do I now hate Ochoa? Let us just say that I feel a personal sense of betrayal.

And I also say my goodbyes to my man in America, as he does the right thing, getting the boat back home. Because no man should be exposed to the kind of suffering that awaits him if, at some future date, with his monkey down, he has to look at another Turk celebrating madly as he scores in added time of extra time.

So I will go on alone.

I will carry on, as that great alcoholic F. Scott Fitzgerald put it in *The Great Gatsby*, boats against the current, borne back ceaselessly into the past.

23 June 2008

- 🌑 100 on Ferrer to beat Gicquel @ 1/3 – **Win**
- 🌑 135 on Karlovic to beat Verdasco @ 4/11 – **Win**
- ⚐ 100 on Kaymer to win BMW tournament in-running @ 1/2 – **Win**
- ⚽ 180 on Spain to qualify against Italy @ 7/10 – **Win**
- ♏ 65 on Somerset to beat Surrey @ 4/7 – **Win**
- 🌑 100 on Ferrero to beat Querrey @ 4/5 – **Win**
- 🌑 180 on Bondarenko to beat Kashiwara @ 1/6 – **Win**
- 🌑 110 on Kuznetsova to beat Johannson in-running @ 4/9 – **Win**
- 🌑 360 on Seppi to beat Kamke @ 1/8 – **Win**

. . . Even

A Bit of Previous
GETTING IT BACK AT THE PARK ON SATURDAY

'JUST WHEN I thought I was out . . . they suck me back in,' said Michael Corleone in *The Godfather*.

Winning back that 500 in two days, with nine straight winners, I also think of the words of my racing mentor Frank O'Neill, on one of the days he brought me and my friend Paul to Dundalk races. Which turned into a very bad day for all of us, a day of losers. And afterwards, we were collected by the excellent Mrs Una O'Neill, who, as she drove us home, could tell from our demeanour that we had 'done' our money.

'How did you do?' she asked perkily, as if her

cheerful tone of voice could somehow restore our spirits.

'Lost fifty quid,' Frank replied gruffly.

At which point the normally even-tempered Una emitted a high-pitched cry of pain.

'Fifty quid?!' she exclaimed. 'Fifty quid?! I have to feed a family . . .'

But before she could continue with all the other things she had to do with that fifty quid which no longer existed, Frank turned to her and, in a tone of voice which he must have thought was reassuring, uttered the following line: 'It's OK. We'll get it back at the Park on Saturday.'

At this, Una emitted an even more high-pitched cry, one of terrible, inconsolable despair. As if she doubted Frank's ability to pick winners at our favourite track, Phoenix Park.

So when I clocked up those nine straight winners, winning back 500 in two days, thirty years after that sad ride home from the races, I would put it like this:

I got it back at the Park on Saturday.

4 July 2008

- 100 on Keothavong to beat King @ 10/11 – **Win**
- 90 on Davydenko to beat Becker @ 4/9 – **Lose**
- 200 on Klaybanova to beat Obzidel @ 2/9 – **Win**
- 160 on Stosur to beat Vaidisova @ 1/5 in-running – **Lose**
- 145 on Ferrero to beat Zverev @ 4/11 – **Lose**
- 140 on Lopez to beat Karanusic @ 2/7 – **Win**
- 200 on Ivanovic to beat Dechy in-running @ 1/3 – **Win**
- 100 on Ochoa to win US Open @ 7/4 – **Lose**
- 100 on Nadal to win Wimbledon @ 7/4 – **Win**
- 100 on Shiavone to beat Medina Garrigues @ 4/5 – **Lose**
- 100 on Mirza to beat Martinez Sanchez @ 4/7 – **Lose**
- 140 on Spain to qualify against Russia @ 8/15 – **Win**
- 100 on Mathieu to beat Chardy @ 4/11 – **Win**
- 110 on Lopez to beat Reynolds @ 2/7 – **Win**
- 140 on Mathieu to beat Cilic @ 8/11 – **Lose**
- 100 on Larrazabal to win French Open @ 8/15 in-running – **Win**
- 100 on Spain to beat Germany @ 4/7 – **Win**
- 110 on Ancic to beat Verdasco @ 4/9 – **Win**
- 100 on Kuznetzova to beat Radwanska @ 10/11 – **Lose**
- 160 on Schuettler to beat Tipsarevic @ 4/9 in-running – **Win**
- 100 on Gasquet to beat Murray @ 5/6 – **Lose**
- 110 on Dementieva to beat Petrova @ 4/7 – **Win**
- 95 on Vaidisova to beat Zheng @ 9/4 in-running– **Lose**
- 100 on India to beat Pakistan @ 4/7 – **Lose**
- 100 on India to beat Sri Lanka @ 8/13 – **Win**
- 60 on LA Dodgers to beat Houston Astros @ 4/6 – **Win**
- 110 on Durham to beat Kent @ 8/11 – **Lose**
- 90 on Garcia in three-ball @ 4/6 – **Win**

- ⬤ 100 on New Zealand to beat South Africa @ 1/3 – **Win**
- ⬤ 50 on S. Williams to beat V. Williams @ 8/11 – **Lose**
- ♏ 85 on Essex to beat Yorkshire @ 4/9 – **Win**
- ━━ 100 on Boston to beat Minnesota @ 8/15 – **Win**
- ♏ 100 on Essex to beat Northants @ 4/6 – **Win**
- ♏ 100 on Lancashire to beat Middlesex @ 4/6 – **Lose**
- ⬤ 100 on Safin to beat Starace @ 8/15 – **Lose**
- ⬤ 55 on Safarova to beat Groenefeld @ 8/11 – **Lose**
- ♏ 270 on Kent to beat Warwickshire @ 4/6 – **Win**
- ⬤ 30 on Karlovic to beat Hanescu @ 2/5 – **Lose**
- ♏ 270 on England to beat South Africa @ 4/9 – **Lose**
- ⚑ 155 on McDowell to beat Khan @ 4/5 – **Win**
- ⬤ 100 on Becker to beat Pless @ 2/5 – **Win**
- ⬤ 100 on Gremelmayer to beat Mayer @ 2/5 – **Lose**

. . . –500

A MOMENT OF SOBER REFLECTION
'IT'S A FAIR COP, GUV, BUT SOCIÉTÉ IS TO BLAME'

IRELAND HAS NOW officially gone into recession.

I'm experiencing something of a downturn myself, a few 'headwinds', but we'll get to that.

Partly the demise of Ireland has been due to oil prices and the credit crunch and so forth, which are driving much of the world into recession, though in our case there has also been a property crash.

And as you walk down the streets of a town like Arklow or Swords, you will see that nearly everything is closing down. Everything apart from gambling dens of various kinds. Not just the myriad betting offices, but casinos too, which are still not properly regulated in Ireland, because we are averse to that sort of thing. But increasingly you can hear it said by respectable people that a well-run casino sector, along with a piece of the global internet betting action, could give old Ireland something of a lift in these troubled times.

Everyone's a winner, baby!

And clearly Ireland, with its vast gambling heritage, its recent successes in so many areas of computer technology, and its existing role as a corporate tax haven, could hardly be better placed to ride this one through.

But the Greens are in government, and in their paternalistic middle-class way they will strive to save the lower orders from their own worst impulses. They have found it hard to convince the lumpen-proletariat that they'd be better off having a nice self-catering family holiday in Waterford, getting there by train, or even hiking, than flying to sunny Spain, doing all that damage to themselves and to the ozone layer. But the Greens would fancy themselves to block even the most sensible gambling initiatives, due to a combination of their own moralistic fervour and the power of the addiction industry in general.

Certainly within seconds of any proposal to crank up Ireland's presence in the international 'gaming' marketplace, a fleet of taxis would be on their way out to the RTE studios, bringing all manner of addiction experts and caring professionals to warn that we are going down the wrong road here, and that no amount of free money from the gaming industry should fool the government into taking this easy option – in the long run, it will cost the Exchequer far more in terms of men withering and lives ruined.

They will also throw in 'concerns' about online betting (in fact any sort of betting) as a form of money-laundering – and there is something in this too.

Against this, I am reminded of that first photo-opportunity taken by Brian Cowen as leader of Fianna Fáil, which pictured him at the counter of the Tullamore branch of Paddy Power with a bunch of fifty-euro notes in his paw, having his Saturday punt.

Such a man won't need a working-party-standing-committee-task-force to tell him that there's money to be made here, by a government that badly needs money, fast.

He might also see a certain symmetry in the fact that the global 'downturn' has been largely caused by what can only be described as gambling, on a gargantuan scale, so maybe gambling should also get us out of it.

The sub-prime racket, the price of oil driven up by speculators, the banks backing the property boom and losing big, the stock markets: what is all this but greedy fuckers gambling in the worst possible way – with other people's money?

Jérôme Kerviel with his own personal 'downturn' of five billion at Société Générale was only following

a certain corporate logic to its ultimate conclusion;
he wasn't doing anything that was essentially alien to
the culture in which he lived. He could say, hand on
heart, 'It's a fair cop, guv, but Société is to blame.'

So when I kicked off this journal with a few
reflections on his plight I was aware that my own
gambling tale was being mirrored on a grand scale by
the machinations of those in the financial services
sector. I felt that this would be an interesting time to
be writing about gambling on every level.

And yet I underestimated the scale of the develop-
ing catastrophe. I did not think that at the end of this
my own finances might be in better shape than those
of the Bradford & Bingley itself.

Today I need only scan the newspapers to see the
following: Wachovia, the fourth largest US bank, was
expected to announce losses of $2.8 billion for the
year. It came out at a loss of $8.8 billion, for the
second quarter of the year . . . Irish banks have 16
billion euros tied up in the US mortgage sector, an
exposure that is much higher than previously
thought . . . Fannie Mae and Freddie Mac, which I
had never heard of until yesterday, are down a few
gazillion, which raises the question of Curly Wee and
Gussie Goose or some other colossal institution
which none of us ever heard of, until it's reported to
be collapsing and taking the United States of
America down with it . . . so isn't it a pity then that
the world economy isn't run by Michael O'Leary of
Ryanair, who is routinely named by almost every
well-known Irish person as the man who should be
running the country, in the way that footballers in

Shoot magazine used to say that they most wanted to meet Muhammad Ali?

Yes, you would think that O'Leary could sort it all out, not today, not tomorrow, but yesterday. But this time even O'Leary is holding a fistful of beaten dockets, with shares in Ryanair losing about a billion in value. And there is much morose reflection on that decision of O'Leary's to which we have already alluded, his failure to 'hedge' when oil was a lot cheaper. On this, one of the bad calls of the epoch, the Ryanair chief executive Michael Cawley gives us the line that the price of oil is just 'a guessing game'.

Good one there, Michael.

It strikes me that that would be a good title for this very tract, or for any work on the nature of gambling – The Guessing Game.

More like The Crying Game, baby!

And what in the name of God is this? In the *Sunday Independent*, alongside a piece by Shane Ross, there's a picture of the billionaire Sean Quinn with the caption: 'Every gossip on the stock market knew that Sean Quinn had been punting – and punting big – on Anglo Irish Bank.'

Now you will remember Sean Quinn as the man who is famous for punting small in his weekly poker game. Back then I saw Sean's bets of 50 cents on the Tuesday night card game in which no one could win anything more than a fiver, as the perfect illustration of the idea that the primal energies of gambling can be released regardless of the size of the pot, that a man can derive just as much satisfaction from winning the fiver as the high roller gets from his big-swinging-mickey exploits.

And now, of all people, my man Sean is being mentioned in these daily dispatches from the economic disaster zone.

Ross writes: 'Sean was rumoured to have bought millions of shares in Anglo. He did not take the normal route. He heard about the cool, modern dealing method – Contracts For Difference (CFDs), which are a mad means of betting big without putting up the money.

'CFD punters typically deposit a 10th of the cost of the shares, borrow the balance, throw the dice and take their chances. They can easily double their money. Or just as easily they can lose the lot. Sean lost. Big time.'

The number being bandied about was a billion. But of course, it's the principle of the thing.

In the world of high finance in general men have been straying from first principles. In the world of 'sub-prime', for example, there are men who apparently forgot the basic proposition that if you lend money you need to have some vaguely reasonable expectation of getting it back some day. Otherwise, you are taking a pretty wild punt there.

Likewise, in a world of endless credit and push-button betting, the sportsman can lose touch with the dirty realism of the old-style betting offices where you had to hand your cash across the counter, perhaps never to be seen again.

Somehow, you feel less of an attachment to plastic money than to the real stuff. Which is not unlike what happens when ordinary folk start getting into the property game, and they start to drift away from that concept of a house as a place where you live, viewing it instead as something on which you speculate in order to accumulate.

Again, by losing touch with the old dirty realism, folk can find themselves speculating more than they ever imagined, and accumulating nothing but a big bad debt to our good friends at the Bradford & Bingley – if it's still out there.

And so it goes, as we look for the shot of adrenalin that gambling can bring, be it a few shillings on the last race at Ballinrobe or an 'investment' of 350 grand on an apartment in Bulgaria.

Yes, some day we will be able to laugh at all that, at the rush of blood which made a crack at the Bulgarian property market seem like the smart play. But if Ireland decides that it would prefer to get through this recession not through gambling but through hard work, through savings and wise investments, perhaps that decision will be influenced by one piece of information in particular contained in Paul Cullen's *Irish Times* feature on gambling.

This had a headline suggesting that one in three compulsive gamblers is female.

Now, I just don't believe that headline figure, if it refers to gambling of the type which mainly interests us here – sports betting. In fact it is clearly ridiculous to suggest that one in three compulsive gamblers on football or racing or cricket or golf is female.

But, according to a Kathryn Holmquist report, our friend the internet has been working its magic in more traditional female markets, such as bingo. Since many women then graduate from bedroom bingo to card games such as Texas Hold Em and poker, online bingo can be likened to an 'entry-level drug'.

While I would hesitate to describe bingo as a form of gambling at all – it is too brainless and sociable for that – when it is being done in private by one person online, rather than in public by a busload of old ladies, it assumes a different character.

And the industry may think it is being very clever with its 'entry-level drug'. It may be trying to make that ultimate breakthrough whereby gambling becomes a form of family entertainment, with father punting on the football match on TV, and mother playing her bingo in the bedroom before graduating to the higher realms of Texas Hold Em, taught to her by their teenage son, who will shortly be flying to Vegas to represent Ireland in the World Poker Championship.

In this idyllic vision of the future, no longer will we have those traditional scenes of the male indulging his guilty addiction, dragging his family down into destitution in his well-meaning but ultimately disastrous pursuit of winners, with the unfortunate children hungry and the long-suffering female essentially in a policing role. Now, in this age of equality, there will also be equality of guilt.

Ah yes, the industry may think it is being very clever here, but perhaps it is forgetting one of the fundamental truths: since the dawn of time the natural enemy of the bookmaker is Woman.

In sports betting, as we have demonstrated, she

has historically failed to grasp the urgent necessity to give back whatever she has won. And now, in her more natural domain of bingo and cards, she may be the rock on which it all perishes, this thing of ours. Because as soon as women start getting addicted to online gambling in significant numbers, then and only then will the whole world feel this terrible pressure to do something about it.

America, France, Germany and Holland have already felt the need to ban online gambling for various reasons pertaining to the good of society, but if it starts to create problems pertaining to the health and welfare of large numbers of women . . . at the mere thought of it, you can already sense the enthusiasm of Irish legislators waning, as they long for the jobs and revenue which gambling can provide but fear the backlash.

Suicide in men, after all, has for long been accepted as an unfortunate fact of life, almost a national pastime. Suicide in women, especially suicide related to gambling, would cause a terrible clamour to *do something*.

The lives of women are widely regarded as being more inherently valuable, perhaps because women are seen as being more virtuous, on the whole, than men – perhaps because they are – so if this internet gambling is catching so many women in its maw, it is powerful shit indeed.

'Mother of Four Commits Suicide Over Gambling Debts' is the sort of headline that could reverse all the hard work put in by the industry to make itself look normal. And we probably won't be seeing such a headline in the realm of sports betting any time soon, but we may well see it in the realm of online bingo. In fact it is inevitable.

'You can chat while you play,' is the advertising line, without the traditional constraints of a busload of other women, chatting and playing for a limited time in a social setting.

But as I mused on these dangers that await our internet providers, and fretted for their safe passage through this world of women, my eye was caught by another piece in the *Irish Times* feature, an interview with an Irish professional poker player who says that the skill lies in winning as much as possible when you have a good hand, and losing as little as possible when you have a bad one.

I am 500 down again in my campaign, sinking all the time in my own estimation. Yet I felt emboldened by this spiel of the poker player, because it sounds like a restatement of my eternal verity – that backing winners is not in itself the problem, the problem is maximizing your winnings by having the right stake at the right time.

And though I have tried, in my way, with that monkey on Croatia, and that 400 on Karlsson and 400 on Tiger, most of these bigger plays have gone down by the tightest of margins.

But I have tried to follow my core beliefs . . . and I must keep trying. Of the numerous winners I have had, if these three bets alone had gone the other way I would be laughing, ahead by miles instead of bobbing above and below the break-even mark.

Instead of eyeing that big prize of a pair of shoes,

or better still a week's wages, I would be thinking that I could nearly be paying the rent with this fine sport, a thought which is doubtless in the heads of other men as they prepare themselves to face this Great Depression.

Yes, that would be a fine thing – to ride out the bad times, betting online, living on your wits.

And as Tony Soprano might put it, this thing of ours is recession proof. Because the oldest working definition of a gamble is when you bet more than you can afford. So if you couldn't afford it in good times, you still can't afford it – but you'll still do it, somehow.

Because you'll have the good days to keep you sane.

Like the Wimbledon final, won magnificently by Nadal, who disappointed me somewhat earlier in the season but who has paid me back handsomely, as I knew he would when he got the old juices running. He has helped me to forget, too, all that I have lost at Wimbledon and at Roland Garros, both of which I entered with such optimism only to be beaten out the door.

So many winners . . . Spain obliged a few times at Euro 2008 . . . but how to make the most of them, now that the collapsing economy has given a new urgency to the task?

So many winners and, yes, a few losers . . . A year ago I backed Andy Roddick who was leading by two sets and a break, and who managed to lose to Richard Gasquet. Last week I backed Richard Gasquet who was leading by two sets and a break, and who managed to lose to my old buddy Andy Murray. Thanks for that, Andy.

If I'd had a gun I'd have shot the television, likewise after my cruel loss on Ferrero, who pulled up lame. And from Lorena Ochoa, the final insult.

Yes, I have discussed this matter with my friend the sportswriter Dion Fanning, and we agree that shooting the television is one of those things we would like to do before we die. We feel it would be quite satisfying, after a particularly ugly defeat, to let off a few rounds, to kill that fucking television. To feel that we were not just sitting there consumed by impotent rage, but that we were hitting back.

Too many losers, some of them quite perverse, quite unacceptable . . . Yet so much has been learned, and we are down just a few hundred, which feels like nothing really – though it is not actually nothing, that's what it feels like. The equivalent of a day at the races, with a meal and drinks and maybe a few pints of petrol on the way home. And a tip of, maybe, 200 to the waiter. An allowable expense.

With a couple of months still to go in this great experiment, I must move on to the next phase, and give it One Last Big Push.

17 July – The British Open starts today

Sergio Garcia will win the British Open some day. But not when my money is on him.

Yet I feel the need to keep backing him, for fear of missing out – though I know eventually that one year I will stop backing him, and then he will win. Maybe next year. It's that old catch-22.

But my annual disappointment in Garcia has become a sort of traditional penance which I am willing to pay for the deep pleasure of partaking of the Open. Like that guy in County Offaly betting on Barack Obama to win Florida, watching Sky News and waiting for the boxes to be opened in Tallahassee, when I throw my usual hundred away on Sergio and see them this morning teeing it up at Royal Birkdale, I know that the world is the best that it has ever been.

1 August 2008

⚑ 100 on Garcia to win British Open @ 8/1 – **Lose**

⚑ 100 on Harrington to win British Open @ 11/4 in-running – **Win**

⚑ 100 on Harrington to beat Norman @ 1/2 – **Win**

200 on Evans to win Tour de France @ 8/13 – **Lose**

🎾 100 on Minar to beat A. N. Other @ 4/6 – **Lose**

⚑ 50 on Weir in three-ball @ 13/8 – **Win**

⚑ 130 on Weir in three-ball @ 11/8 – **Lose**

⚽ 100 on Young Boys to beat Basle @ 8/15 in-running – **Lose**

🎾 100 on Querrey to beat Reynolds @ 4/9 – **Win**

⚑ 100 on Harrington to beat Duval @ 4/7 – **Win**

Ⓜ 120 on South Africa to beat England @ 1/6 – **Win**

🎾 45 on Gasquet to beat Llodra @ 1/2 – **Win**

●— 60 on Part to beat Mason @ 2/5 – **Win**

Ⓜ 60 on Durham to beat Glamorgan @ 1/3 – **Win**

🎾 85 on Roddick to beat Mahut 1/6 – **Win**

🏇 20 on Duke Of Marmalade @ 4/6 – **Win**

Ⓜ 30 on Kent to beat Middlesex @ 4/5 – **Lose**

⚑ 180 on Cook to beat Vaughan @ 8/11 – **Lose**

— 100 on New York Mets to beat St Louis Cardinals @ 1/2 – **Win**

— 50 on Oakland Athletics to beat Texas Rangers @ 4/5 – **Win**

— 100 on Boston Red Sox to beat NY Yankees @ 1/2 – **Win**

— 50 on Toronto Blue Jays to beat Tampa Bay Rays @ 4/5 – **Win**

🎾 270 on Nadal to beat Kiefer in straight sets @ 2/11 – **Win**

. . . −630

Deposit: 1,000

So I backed the winner of the British Open after all. I took a piece of that 11/4 on Harrington 'in-running', on the Sunday.

And yet at this point the addiction therapist will be suggesting an 'intervention'. Here am I, a man who started off a few short months ago with a deposit of 100, now considerably behind and depositing ten times that, and still clinging to the hope of ultimate triumph. At this rate – they will insist – by Christmas I will be making regular deposits of ten grand, and let the devil take the hindmost.

Will I not now stop? Or will I have to be stopped?

To which I say, ah fuck it, you know? I'm about 600 down overall on the Free Money account, which means that this thing has been costing me about 30 euros a week. Which means that I'd be paying more than twice as much to an addiction therapist for a service which is available just once a week, for an hour, instead of 24/7/365 worldwide.

And for that outlay I wouldn't have had the inexpressible joy of backing the winners of the US Open, the Champions League final, Wimbledon, and now the British Open.

I used to live across the wall from the family home of Padraig Harrington in Rathfarnham, an 'omen' which has cost me dear for a long time. And like me, Harrington has a brother who happens to be a bookie, another of those expensive co-incidences. And moreover I announced back in 2002 on an RTE Radio programme that Harrington was the next Nick Faldo and would win at least six majors, a bold statement in which I fully believed, which only ramped up my losses year-on-year on my old neighbour.

Yet when I had that 100 on Padraig at 11/4 on the last day of the Open, winning back just a small proportion of what I have lost on him, it still gave me a blast of joy, and a sense of ownership – this, after all, was my fifth major, having already 'won' a

Masters and two USPGAs and this year's US Open with Tiger.

And here is the best part: I was able to enjoy a day at the beach with my wife and daughter while the last round was being played. Taking extreme care not to hear the result, we got home around seven o'clock. And then we watched TV for the evening. Not the Open, which I had recorded on Sky Plus, just the usual Sunday evening stuff. And then, at the end of the sort of family day so beloved of the traditionalists, I watched the whole of Harrington's winning round on Sky Plus.

Round midnight, he was getting the better of Greg Norman. Then for a while Ian Poulter appeared determined to wreck my buzz. But at about two in the morning, Harrington hit another perfect drive down the fairway of the seventeenth, a par five. And then I watched him hitting that stupendous five-wood on to the green, about 4 feet from the hole. He would not be stopped now.

I watched all this 'as live'. And it was sublime.

No therapist could give me that. Nor could I see the therapist whenever I liked, 'as live'. Nor could I stop seeing the therapist whenever I liked – there is so much work to be done, the therapist would tell me, and she would probably be right.

But can I stop betting whenever I like?

In truth, despite my high strike rate, and for all my gallows humour, I am thinking about it. I have not yet reached for the white flag, but I know where it is, if I need it.

In more academic circles they might call this a radical paradigm shift.

My deposit of 1,000 (perhaps my most successful deposit yet) is now down to 830, which is no big deal. And yet, while it is a cause of some personal sadness, it offers a textbook illustration of what we are up against here.

Above, I have recorded twenty-four bets, of which sixteen

were winners, including four in a row on baseball – and I don't even know the rules of baseball – and that bet on Harrington, another good day at the office there. So how could I not be ahead?

One bet . . . out of twenty-four . . . Just one bet has done me down, leaving me on the wrong side of the margin. Maybe it was that naïve 200 on Cadel Evans to win the Tour de France (he finished second); or that appalling 100 on Young Boys Berne to beat Basle in-running, a moment of deep insanity in the midst of so much honest toil.

But what disturbs me most about these figures is the fact that if I were over there with the boys in Alderney, running my internet betting empire, I would be regarding the likes of me as a most desirable client. I am good enough to back a load of winners, which keeps me coming back, despite the losers, like Pavlov's dog. But I'm not good enough to make it count.

At least . . . not yet.

If I were just completely useless, it is the boys in Alderney who would ultimately have a problem, because by now I would have gone through the 1,000, and I might well have reached for that white flag, giving up in total disgust and despair. But I'm still hanging in there, because of that winning feeling – sixteen times out of twenty-four I get that winning feeling, two times out of three, yet despite that winning feeling I'm losing in the end, and it's bringing me down.

So I have mused much on the need to win big when you win, and to lose small when you lose. I have spoken movingly on the need to bet less. And to bet more. And yet, as these latest figures illustrate so profoundly, I have too rarely followed my own advice, probably because my punting life on the whole has primarily been a quest for pleasure, not profit – which has prevented me from arriving at a true understanding of the bet less/bet more conundrum.

I understand it in theory, but in practice I have been found wanting. I guess I've been afraid that the bet less/bet more conundrum will turn into a bet more/bet more situation ... with consequences too terrible to contemplate.

So it is not my strong suit. But do I have a strong suit?

Well, on all the evidence so far, my strongest suit is what I have called 'getting it back at the Park on Saturday'.

On several occasions I have dug myself out of a hole with a series of winners which bring me roughly back to break-even. At which point I get a bit excited and I start having fun again with a few bigger bets, and soon I'm back where I started, in clawback mode.

For some twisted reason, 'getting it back at the Park on Saturday' seems to concentrate the mind like no other proposition. And the psychology here is revealing. Because it brings into play the punter's lack of self-esteem, the fact that he ends up being delighted to break even, or to lose just a small amount.

As we say in Ireland, if you're expecting a kick in the balls, you're happy enough with a slap in the face.

In fact it is not unknown for punters to feel a certain glow of achievement when an event is cancelled and the bet is void, and they get their money back.

Clearly I am not as focused when I am trying to surge ahead as I am in the hole, with a shovel in my hand. So if I can somehow fool myself into believing that I am always behind, always trying to get it back at the Park on Saturday ... come to think of it, that would not require a great feat of self-deception.

Is this the radical paradigm shift that I need?

Certainly I must keep reminding myself that clawback is my

strong suit, but should it be worn at all times or only on special occasions?

I suspect that as this journey moves ominously closer to the Olympic Games in China, the land of a billion gamblers, my powers will be tested like never before.

5 August 2008

- 100 on Henry The Navigator @ 2/5 – **Win**
- 110 on Isner to beat Stoppini @ 4/11 – **Win**
- 70 on South Africa to beat England @ 4/7 – **Win**
- 90 on Mickelson to win WGC Invitational @ 5/2 – **Lose**
- 100 on Kerry to beat Monaghan @ 1/3 – **Win**
- 190 on USA to win most gold medals at Olympics @ 13/8 – **Unsettled**
- 410 on USA to win most gold medals at Olympics @ 2/1 – **Unsettled**

. . . −565

8 August 2008 – The Olympics start today

And I realize the time indeed has come to consider my portfolio for Beijing.

Now, in considering one's portfolio for a programme of events of which one knows nothing, events that feature ten thousand names one has never heard of before, one might arrive at the conclusion that the best portfolio here is to have no portfolio at all.

Alas, I am human.

And so I do something that I will probably regret. In fact . . . I'm regretting it already.

I have 600 on the USA to win the most gold medals, 190 at 13/8 and another 410 at what seems like the excellent price of 2/1. Or to be precise I have 188 at 13/8, all the eights there for a bit of that good Chinese luck.

It all seemed excellent until approximately five seconds after I pressed the 'bet now' button, when I began to regard it as a near-certain loser.

How did I do it?

Well, I followed the market, and in so doing, against all my better instincts, I think I started looking for the 'value'. And USA at 2/1 is certainly the value. China, which a week ago was 4/7 and is now 4/11, is not the value.

But why is it now 4/11? Could it be connected in any way to the fact that China will almost certainly win the most gold medals? Maybe . . . maybe so.

So how did I do it? How did I dig myself this fresh hole, after all we've been through?

Well, my thinking here will at least serve as an educational tool.

I got carried along on a train of thought which went something like this: since the Games haven't started yet, and the price of China is still tumbling down, there must be vast amounts of money going on them, and very little money going on the USA. So where is all this money coming from?

Well, sad to say, a certain percentage of it would be coming from the shrewdies who have figured that the Olympics is all about cheating, and that being the case, China is bound to prevail.

But a high percentage may be coming from Chinese people themselves, betting their brains out in patriotic fervour – certainly there'd be more money coming from the oriental diaspora than from the USA, where internet betting is illegal.

In this version, perhaps that increasingly skinny price is more reflective of nationalistic sentiment than of the real state of the parties. Indeed I am told that there's a man in this country who made fifty grand last year entirely on the premise that Andy Murray's opponents are usually a longer price with the British bookies than they should be, due to all the 'patriotic' money going on Andy.

Clever, no?

And in assessing the astuteness of all that Chinese money, I reflected on the fact that every day, in every betting office in every town in Ireland, you will find members of that oriental diaspora betting like men. Betting on anything that moves, and on a lot of things that hardly move at all, on the all-weather tracks of Wolverhampton and Great Leighs.

So when these guys are gung-ho, maybe it's time for the more sober individual to take heed and take advantage?

Yeah, maybe it is.

Unfortunately, maybe the time is not now, I told myself, with the money down, the deal done. When it was too late. Because you can't change your mind once you have pressed the 'bet now' button. At that stage of the game, even a woman is not permitted to change her mind.

And now all I can see in the mind's eye is a horde of Chinese divers and ping-pong players standing on the podium receiving their gold medals and weeping uncontrollably.

I, who have been charting the disintegration of American power from Bear Stearns to Fannie Mae and Freddie Mac, I, of all people, felt that the USA was still worthy of my investment – for a few moments at least.

And as a result, I am going to get burned.

Knowing this, I am still afflicted by a sort of paralysis that prevents me from having a 'saver' on China, because at the current odds that would mean having about two grand on China. And at this stage I feel that my instincts in this bullshit market have gone so completely awry, it would be quite possible for the Americans to do it after all, thus costing me about a grand in winnings wiped out by my own hand, which is the sort of thing that makes men mad, quite irretrievably mad.

No, I have made my big mistake, and as a matter of policy I don't think it wise to follow a mistake of this magnitude with a bet of two grand on anything. Because if you go down that road, even if it works the first time, there will surely come a time when it won't work. And that will be a very, very bad time, a time when you will come to know the true meaning of words like 'slippery' and 'slope'.

Now you will note that what I am doing here is exactly the opposite of what most tipsters do every day, when they tell you exactly why their selections are going to win.

I'm telling you why I am going to lose.

But then I think there should be more of this. Because from an early age I made it my business to reread the tipsters in the morning papers as I journeyed home from a day at the races.

Ah, it was such poignant stuff, all that hope now turned to nothing, all the morning's wisdom looking like such a waste of time and money.

Hemingway used to regard reading the 'form' in the papers as a true illustration of the art of fiction, but perhaps we only grasp its fictional essence when we read it after the event. Only then does it fully acquire all those layers of sadness, only in rereading do we truly feel the futility of the struggle.

In this vein I should emphasize that the exact stake on the USA at 13/8 was not 190 but 188, due to the fact that 8 is the lucky number of these Games. And again it was only afterwards that I heard the baleful gods whispering darkly to me that 8 is indeed a lucky number . . . for the Chinese. Not for Paddy.

Never for Paddy.

And in my gloom, with another big play about to go down, I was further saddened by a change in the layout and colour scheme of the Blue Square website.

Way back, I explained that I gave my business to Blue Square because I preferred the colour blue to the horrible green of Paddy Power. It seemed to suit my eye.

Now, inexplicably, they have added these fatal bands of green. I hate it.

I hate myself for putting my tank on Team USA and now I hate this green thing, which destroys the blue elegance of the old livery, and which I half-suspect was introduced as a sop to poor Paddy, and all he has lost.

This here Paddy is not having it.

I am moving to Boylesports.

And while I realize that the announcement will not be appearing in the appointments section of the business pages of the *Irish Times*, there is more to this move than mere pique.

Boylesports, according to itself, was founded in Armagh. And it is particularly strong in the border regions. And it is there that this sporting life began for me.

Frank O'Neill and many of his racing buddies were from Armagh. Perhaps they did battle with some ancestor of Boyle, and now it has fallen to me to take up the cudgels. Perhaps my memories of those proud beginnings, when I was no more than a child, taking on the bookies of Bandit Country, will inspire me in the home straight, on the way to Valhalla.

Of course I am wondering too if this is where the journey will end for me. Or if the 'radical paradigm shift' of which I speak involves no more than a shift from Blue Square to Boylesports.

I might have switched to Paddy Power too, for the equally good reason that Power himself is a person known to me from his many media appearances, someone at whom I can direct all my hostility, perhaps sharpening my performance in the process.

But Paddy Power isn't offering anything like the 200 in free bets you get as a signing-on fee with Boylesports, partly I suspect because Paddy figures he can rope the punters in anyway, through his ubiquitous media presence, and all that fine bullshit.

And so I prepare to take on the boys of County Armagh.

12 August 2008

ᛗ	50 on Warwickshire to beat Northants @ 4/6 – **Win**
◖	90 on Fish to beat Spadea @ 1/2 – **Win**
⚐	50 (free bet) on Garcia to be leading European @ 6/1 – **Lose**
⚐	90 on a USA player to win USPGA @ 6/5 – **Lose**
⚐	90 on Vijay Singh in three-ball @ 8/13 – **Lose**
⬥	50 (free bet) on Germany to win the Aga Khan Cup @ 15/8 – **Lose**
⚐	120 on Holmes to beat Wi @ 4/5 – **Win**

...–560

After a bout of intense hostilities, there is stalemate. But I have to grudgingly admire my latest adversary, Boylesports, for the deep cleverness of their Free Bet system.

Like all things that lure men to their doom, at first sight it seems mighty seductive. It looks like they're doing you a favour, that they're being quite foolishly big-hearted in their appreciation of your business, to the extent that you feel a pang of guilt that you're taking advantage of them, these poor desperate men.

Instead of the usual paltry 20 or 25 quid offer, there's the big number 200. And that number is not a lie, they really do give you 200 in free bets. And that number doesn't get any smaller on closer examination.

Ah, but it is not the size, it is the structure of the thing that is so fine.

The boys of County Armagh have structured this in such a sophisticated way, it makes the efforts of the boys in Alderney look almost naïve. It demonstrates a supreme clarity of purpose.

You get the first free 50 after the first bet, which itself must be at least 50. So 50 is the new 20 here, a subtle raising of the bar. And you get the next 50 only after you have had five more bets which average at least 50 – they will also match your stake if you want to bet smaller, but human nature being what it is – particularly human nature when it is interacting with a sports betting website – you will tend to bet the 50 to get the full value of the freebie.

Soon, you will be getting that winning feeling. And in the unlikely event that you back five or six losers straight off, which might conceivably scare you away from gambling as a career choice, you will probably still hang on for the third free 50, and the fourth, so that you'll have had more than fifteen cracks at it before the free money runs out.

If you can walk away at this point, you're a solid and sober citizen and it's hard to understand why a person like you would be on Boylesports dot com in the first place. They don't need your type in the industry of human happiness.

But for normal men who are offered such inducements, there's really no going back.

They're leaving so little to chance here, there's even an amusing little announcement that the free bet is not available to citizens of Russia, Georgia, or the Ukraine.

As to why they are not so appreciative of the business of men in those territories, we can but speculate. But the words 'unusual', 'betting' and 'patterns' suggest themselves.

And we will probably never know the truth of this either, but in all likelihood the vast majority of these free bets go down. Certainly that free 50 I had on Sergio Garcia at 6/1 to be the leading European in the USPGA championship went down, but it was worth having a crack in the circumstances. I would not have backed Garcia in this tournament with bad money of my own, but with free money, and needing to accelerate at this stage of the quest, I thought: why not?

So many men, in this situation, think: why not?

And too late, the answer comes: because you would not do this with your own money, and why not? Because you would almost certainly lose.

Too late that answer comes, always too late.

I am the man who said that Harrington would win six majors, yet I went with Garcia again, thinking that even a man with Harrington's confidence could hardly win two majors in a row. And with Garcia leading by a shot from Harrington with three holes to go, clearly my analysis of the market had been sound. The fact that Garcia then hit his ball into the lake, and missed a short putt on the next hole is not my fault. Again, I can find little wrong with my own performance here; it is Garcia who buggered it up. Except this time, instead of bailing me out as he had done at Birkdale, Harrington snuffed me out.

For the free 50 I had on Germany at 15/8 to win the Aga Khan Cup, the fault is mine.

All mine.

SELF-CONDEMNATION . . . ENVY . . . FALSE PRIDE . . .

I HAVE RECEIVED an email from a compulsive gambler who is unhappy with a piece I wrote in the *Sunday Independent* about the licensing of casinos in Ireland. As readers of this journal know by now, generally speaking, though I am not particularly interested in casinos on a personal level, I am in favour of legalizing them, as I am in favour of legalizing gambling in general. I am also in favour of legalizing cocaine and heroin, if only because we have clearly seen that making them illegal has brought no benefit whatsoever to mankind, and has probably made the situation far worse by leaving it all to our friends in the organized crime sector.

My email correspondent, being a compulsive gambler, is understandably down on the whole racket, and has no wish to see casinos thriving in a country full of gamblers in these hard times. But he is especially critical of my views on the overall position of the government in relation to gambling. He thinks the government can do more about it; I don't think the government can do much about it.

They may ban the lethal 'fixed-odds betting terminals', and that's fine, but it won't stop any of the prospective patrons of fixed-odds betting terminals finding some other way to 'do' their money.

And this is not an ideological position. It is a view based entirely on hard-won personal experience in relation to alcohol, which taught me many things, not least the fact that no one ever got cured of an addiction because of some measure brought in by the minister. No one ever gave up drinking because of something the government did or said or promised.

It is a discovery that the individual must make for himself. This is not an ideological position – au contraire, I would be a man of the Left – it is a simple statement of what works and what obviously doesn't work. In fact a compulsive gambler would probably be more 'ideological' about it than I am, because of his immersion in Gamblers Anonymous and other programmes of recovery which advise you to get in contact with your Higher Power.

But I treat the views of addicts with much respect, because in the area of addiction, which is teeming with all sorts of bullshitters, the addict himself is one of the few genuine experts.

So while I would lock horns with my email correspondent on several points, I would concede that in this book I have perhaps not reflected greatly on the very darkest horrors of this thing, that circle of hell where we find the ordinary man, the average industrial wage-earner, who has managed to lose maybe a hundred grand, who has already committed many crimes in his desperate pursuit of winners, crimes against humanity and crimes against the law.

To his unfortunate loved ones, and perhaps to himself if he ever turns the corner, I can understand that anything written about gambling which doesn't advocate its immediate eradication, by brute force if necessary, must seem unforgivable.

Because at the end of the road which began with a punt on Big Brother and a free bet of £20, there can be a scene of unimaginable destruction.

Not that it all kicked off with internet gambling.

I have an ancient memory of this little Italian man who was apparently doing very well for himself running the local chippie until, it was said, he lost everything playing poker. I played with his two sons until they were forced to move elsewhere, their fate decided by a game of cards. And even as a child, I understood that something terrible had happened to them, and I felt a sense of awe. I had a mental image of this little Italian, who seemed so vigorous as the boss man of his own thriving business, so hard-working, so powerful, sitting at the card table after losing everything, a vision of powerlessness.

How does it feel?

How does it feel to be walking away from a game of cards and facing the consequences of total ruination?

And yet . . . I also know of an amazing stroke of luck that the same man had around that time.

Once, when I was playing with his sons, the younger one, who was about seven at the time, ran across the road without looking. There was a car coming, and I remember with absolute clarity the moment when I knew for certain that the boy would be killed. And I remember my amazement when the moment passed and the car kept going and there was the boy on the other side of the road, still standing, unharmed.

In all likelihood the boy's father has gone through life never knowing about this amazing stroke of luck. And maybe he's better off that way. Because as a gambler, he would probably have looked at it this way: the baleful gods may have dealt him the wrong cards, which destroyed his business, but perhaps this was their way of softening the blow. Having lost his livelihood, they spared him the ultimate catastrophe of losing his son as well.

Knowing this, he might start feeling lucky again, lucky enough to review his situation. He might feel that he was not after all a doomed individual, that maybe he just caught a bad break, and there was still another game of cards in him, maybe one in which he could get it all back. And if somehow he found himself in that game trying to get it all back, with thousands in the pot . . . how would it feel?

Sometimes, at a particularly tense moment in some deeply dubious tennis match, I wonder what it would be like if I had, say, ten grand resting on the next point, rather than the fifties and hundreds which are more my speed. At this moment of maximum uncertainty, of total surrender to the power of another, I can imagine that other dimension of fear, but I can't imagine myself actually being there.

I am not a professional gambler, who, like a professional in any field, has a certain emotional detachment from the business at hand. I am not mad enough to be the kind of fellow who is relaxed about dropping ten grand as a result of some rich guy missing a short putt, through sheer carelessness.

I don't think I could stand the pain of owing fantastic amounts of money to people well-known to me, like the doctor interviewed in the *Observer* magazine last year, an elder lemon of Gamblers

Anonymous who finally surrendered after many years backing the dogs with money that he would borrow from patients when he couldn't get it anywhere else.

As I recall, it took this highly paid professional about seventeen years to pay it all back, but he did it, once he had truly understood the nature of his madness.

Like the AA programme, GA speaks of the need for a 'daily moral inventory' of the type that seems more appropriate to gamblers than to any other variety of piss-artist or bullshit-artist.

On one side, there are faults to be wary of, such as self-condemnation, envy and false pride. On the other, a list of good things for which to strive, such as self-evaluation, generosity and simplicity.

Ah, it's there, it's all there . . . self-condemnation . . . envy . . . false pride . . . The punter carries these three things within himself, the way that Superman carried the flame of truth, justice and the American way. Self-condemnation . . . envy . . . false pride . . . these are toxins which permeate the punter's body and his soul, and they probably account for that sense of dissipation in every betting office in every town, that powerful smell of male desperation.

Even when they open an office with a water cooler and a coffee machine – and they're doing that all the time in Ireland – within weeks the smell of the fresh paint and the new fittings is gone, and it has that old, old atmosphere of decay and decrepitude which is uniquely created by these daily gatherings of disappointed men.

There's usually a bin for the losing slips, out of which one slip is drawn every week, entitling the owner to a free bet. So one punter can feel lucky again, though there's every chance that his rescued slip will merely give him another little jab of pain, two jabs for the price of one.

And probably the main difference between the small-time loser and the big-time loser is an ability to take the pain. The small-timer can't stand the pain of losing his month's wages, his life savings, his chip shop. He can just about stand the pain of losing fifties and hundreds, because he is a masochist after all, like a drug user who has known pleasure and who keeps trying to get the good stuff back. He is at the lower end of the masochistic scale, whupped so often he has come to enjoy the ritual, numbed into believing that he can eventually play the dominant role, that it's roughly fifty-fifty, though it's not fifty-fifty, even very roughly.

But at the higher end, the big-time loser can take a lot more pain; he is almost a connoisseur of pain, somewhat in the style of an S&M fetishist. We see this when the punter enters one of those 'self-exclusion' programmes, though he still tries to have a bet, hoping to God that the bookie will disregard his own rules about not taking any more bets from compulsive gamblers in this category – it's the equivalent of the S&M freak issuing the classic instruction to the dominatrix: don't stop, no matter what I say, don't stop. So he is stretched on the rack until he can't take it any more, until he is completely broken, until he begs in the most pitiful way for the things which he dreads even more than this medieval torture – self-evaluation, generosity and simplicity.

20 August 2008

♕♕♕   600 on USA to win most gold medals at Olympics – **Lose**

●   50 (free bet) on Berdych/Stepanek to beat Melo/Sa @ 8/11 – **Lose**

ⅲ   100 on Kent to beat Leicestershire @ 1/3 – **Void**

●   265 on Bryan/Bryan to beat Melzer/Knowles @ 1/7 – **Missing**

♕♕♕   100 on Lee/Lee to beat Emms/Robertson @ 5/6 – **Win**

●   130 on Gonzalez to beat Mathieu @ 8/13 – **Win**

♕♕♕   100 on China to beat Japan (volleyball) @ 4/9 – **Win**

▰   50 (free bet) on Censored @ 4/6 – **Win**

●   100 on Wozniak to beat Vakulenko @ 1/2 – **Win**

♕♕♕   120 on China to beat Kazakhstan (handball) @ 1/6 – **Lose**

●   100 on Blake to beat Gonzalez @ 4/6 – **Lose**

●   90 on Djokovic to beat Nadal @ 6/4 – **Lose**

●   150 on Jankovic to beat Safina @ 6/5 – **Lose**

●   210 on Del Potro to beat Isner @ 2/7 – **Win**

♕♕♕   100 on Belarus to win single sculls @ 1/3 – **Lose**

♕♕♕   120 on Great Britain to win coxless fours @ 4/11 – **Win**

⚽   125 on Valencia to draw with Real Madrid @ 8/13 – **Lose**

━   90 on Tampa Bay to beat Texas @ 4/7 – **Win**

. . . –1,350

'Hope is the worst of evils, for it prolongs the torments of Man,' Nietzsche wrote, another man there who must have seen a few cross doubles going down to speak with such authority on that old devil called Hope.

Already I am officially declaring my big play on the USA a loss, like the bookies paying out in August on Stoke City to get relegated. But if there is any consolation for me, watching this Olympics with such profound sadness, it is the fact that all hope was gone even before the start. Otherwise I might have spent these weeks hoping that the USA would prevail, hoping, and hoping against hope.

Thankfully I will be spared that long-festering disappointment, now that the first week in Beijing has confirmed that the Chinese have left nothing to chance here in their maniacal determination to do me down. They are winning three gold medals before breakfast (my breakfast at least) and I am still struggling to understand how I made a fundamental error of such magnitude. I am examining it like a forensic pathologist cutting up the corpse of an old friend.

I can see it happening on five screens simultaneously, the BBC's interactive coverage making this a special time for anyone who likes to watch a bit of clay-pigeon shooting at 6 a.m. on the main screen, with a bit of judo and a bit of rowing and a bit of boxing and a bit of archery on the small screens – it's like Slamtracker with pictures, and like Slamtracker no punter can see such things without being deeply moved.

I have found myself betting on things such as volleyball and handball, and for this I am further consumed by feelings of guilt and shame. But first I must attend to a new darkness which has entered my life since my controversial move to Boylesports.

Apart from the fact that the Boylesports site doesn't suit my eye at all, creating an air of instability in an already unstable atmosphere, I found myself in dispute with them over a bet which didn't seem to register on their system.

A winning bet, of course, on the Bryan brothers to win a tennis doubles match, an exercise in 'buying money' which would have brought me a modest return of about 50 euros.

I felt confident that I had made that bet, so I engaged in a brief email correspondence with 'Colin', one of Boylesports' unfortunate crew, whose days are filled with the garbled missives of unhappy punters, some of whom are doubtless bullshitting.

But I was not bullshitting.

Nor indeed was 'Colin'. And I'm not suggesting here for a moment that there was anything inherently wrong with the Boylesports site. We are all at the mercy of dark technological forces, and doubtless there is some innocent explanation – with the punter's lack of self-esteem, we always suspect that deep down, we are in the wrong.

So 'Colin' offered to leave me in the capable hands of the IT people, though for punting purposes I need hardly add that I was out of there.

For the punter, the mere idea of backing a winner only to be defeated by the technology is quite terrifying, as we contemplate the apocalyptic dread of winning an awful lot more than fifty quid only to have it disappear into the nothingness of cyberspace.

Naturally, it never occurs to us that we might back a big loser only to discover a few minutes later that the stake is still standing there in our account, as if the bet had just been magicked away. We know that that could never happen because . . . we just know these things.

Yes, I will miss the heightened sense of animosity I perhaps unfairly felt towards Boylesports, and I still hate those strips of green on Blue Square, but I am left with no alternative here . . . except Paddy Power. And that would bring to mind a thing that alcoholics call 'doing a geographical', which means deluding yourself that if you move to another city or even another country, you'll be able to get off the drink and start again as a sober and successful person.

Tragically, all the available evidence suggests that you can change your location, you can change your job, you can change your car, you can even change your shoes from time to time, but eventually you must change yourself. And that, as they say in corporate circles when they move their factory from Westmeath to Bangladesh, is location-indifferent.

Ah, but I am in a bad place with my punting, wheresoever it may be.

On this journey, as we well know, four bets of 400 and over have gone down. And that has made all the difference.

But the 400 on Tiger was eminently justifiable. And I got it all back, on the same Tiger. The 400 on Karlsson was beaten by one shot, a bad break. And the 500 lost on Croatia was the worst break in the history of the world.

But 600 on the USA to win more gold medals than China?

I find it hard to let this go. I find it hard to accept that I swallowed the received wisdom, which suggested that the Chinese would win all around them in the little sports, but the USA would be strong in the pool, and score heavily at track and field as they traditionally do. I received this wisdom from several supposedly reliable media sources, as I read myself into this brief.

Of course, it was bullshit.

And it was such bullshit, you'd have to wonder how it got out there at all. Was it just the usual lame-brained hackery, or perhaps something a tad more sinister? Alas, it was probably just the lame-brained hackery, which I can usually see a mile away, but not this time, no sir.

It was quickly apparent that Michael Phelps was strong in the pool, and the rest was mostly Australia. And if Phelpsy had entered a few track and field events on his way home, he could hardly have done worse than Team USA, who had a few fast women, and the rest was mostly Jamaica.

The wisdom that I received made no mention of the possibility that America might be weak where once it was strong, leaving it vulnerable against the totalitarian prowess of Team China.

Which reminds me that I have undoubtedly been cheated by a load of home-town decisions and by an old-fashioned long-term state-sponsored drive to win at all costs. And yes, Tolstoy said that a gentleman is someone who pays his gambling debts, even when he knows he's been cheated, but Tolstoy wasn't cheated by an entire nation, was he?

Yes, I could make excuses, but I will rise above all that. And anyway, if you know you're going to be swindled and you still go there, the shame is on you, baby!

Ah, it sounds completely ridiculous now to have gone against China. I am in awe of how ridiculous it was. But there must be something that we can glean from this, some sliver of insight, assuming that I was not simply mad at the time, or that I have not in fact been mad for some time now without realizing it.

Because there is something else that I forgot to mention in that confident prediction of failure. Maybe my mind had briefly erased it, but it comes back to me now, that for several months I had been planning to back the Chinese. The publisher of this book can verify that six months ago, in general conversation, I told him that a bet on China to win the medals table would be the smart play. And still somehow I bamboozled myself out of it.

We do that all the time.

How do we do it?

We get a few bad breaks, yes, and we think too much, yes, and sometimes we don't think enough. We're just not paying attention.

But like a crowd gathered around a three-card-trick merchant, we are also constantly underestimating how cunning, how baffling, how powerful are these gambling arts.

Yes, we are like that crowd losing their pennies in games of find-the-lady, except they usually dally for a few minutes and then move on, amused and bemused by what they have seen, harrumphing that they won't get fooled again.

We who bet on sports, thinking it is a higher calling, are also suckers for every old routine. But we are worse, because we don't move on, we stay for hours trying to crack the secret of the three-card trick, we stay there for days, for most of our lives.

There is one form of sports betting that is so similar to the three-card trick it should be reviled by all decent people, yet it is enormously popular. This is the three-ball betting in golf, which, like the three-card trick, looks quite easy at first. Instead of finding the winner of the entire tournament, your guy only has to beat two other guys, on the day. And if there's a tie, you still get something back.

Could anything be simpler?

Well, there's the two-ball betting, which looks even simpler than that, like a mere two-card trick until you consider the possibility of a tie, which in their enthusiasm very few punters do. Which actually makes it a slightly sneakier version of the three-ball betting, and which cost me 400 when the accursed Karlsson could only tie with the guy he was supposed to beat by fourteen shots.

So why is that three-ball scam so enormously popular?

I guess there is just some weakness in our nature that makes us vulnerable to the hocus pocus, convinces us we can find the lady, particularly if the lady in question is called Lorena Ochoa.

And sometimes we can find the lady – to keep us going – but to our stupefaction, many times we can't find her. And somehow we never find her when we make our boldest play, moving from the pennies to the folding money.

Always, there is some distraction, some ancient manoeuvre

that makes us lose our concentration for the fraction of a second it takes to send us to the wrong place. We know not the levels of madness in which we are indulging, when we try to arrange the future for personal gain. But madness it is, which begets madness.

'Play The "IF" In Life' is the Boylesports slogan, though eagle-eyed observers may note that there is also a 'LIE' in Life. In fact it is mostly a LIE.

And in our intellectual arrogance we also underestimate the fact that these guys we are up against, in Armagh or in Alderney, are just a lot better than us. So when that price on China started going through the floor, the whole point of the exercise was perhaps to ensnare the likes of me, to cause exactly the reaction that happened. To reel in a load of guys who thought they were being smart, though they knew nothing about most of these Olympic Games, except that crock of received wisdom. To get them thinking a bit, instead of going with their raw instinct. To tempt them into the abyss, exactly – not approximately – but exactly as it happened.

Yes, these guys are a lot better than we are at arranging the future. But really, they are better than they need to be.

And for all these reasons, and a few more to which we have alluded, it becomes the punter's most cherished ambition somehow to break even. That is the Grail. Not to win, not to lose, just to get away with it.

Yes, that is the most Holy Grail.

And it is to be found atop that hill, so one must roll the rock upwards and upwards until that happy day when the job is done. For me, to get that rock up the hill, to seize the Grail by next month, will require a gargantuan effort. I must make at least a grand in that time – and not lose a grand, or two grand – a hard road home, and ideally I wouldn't be starting from here.

A MOMENT OF SOBER REFLECTION
SO MUCH MORE TO BE ANXIOUS ABOUT

I THINK NOW of these words from the auto-biography of Bertrand Russell: 'Three passions, simple but overwhelmingly strong, have governed my life: the longing for love, the search for knowledge, and unbearable pity for the sufferings of mankind. Three passions, like great winds, have blown me hither and thither, in a wayward course over a deep ocean of anguish, reaching to the very verge of despair.'

For sure, Russell must have come out the wrong side of a few photo-finishes at the White City, to speak of life's vicissitudes with such power.

But like Russell, I must move away from my own personal unhappiness to a broader contemplation of the issues. And I am struck by a piece from Beijing by Will Buckley of the *Observer*, a piece from the table-tennis hall which carries an echo of themes we have been exploring in these tear-stained pages.

A game that was about coping with boredom is now all twitches and glitches, concerned with anxiety. This is apt. At the risk of being glib, it is possible to equate totalitarian states with boredom, and capitalist ones with anxiety. Where would the money-makers be without status anxiety, sexual anxiety, social anxiety and all the other sundry anxieties? Pretty anxious, is the answer. There's no money to be made out of people's peace of mind.

In direct opposition, there's the numbing boredom of living in a totalitarian state, the ennui that follows from not being able to do anything about everything. All Olympic disciplines, but particularly perhaps table tennis – for shy people are nothing if not anxious – combine the boredom of practising all day every day for four years, with the performance anxiety of it being over in minutes . . .

Yes, gamblers can relate to these observations, because they recognize that what they do is akin to ping-pong, a response to boredom and to the anxiety which it creates. It seems that the more entertainment we are given, the more bored we get. And so the anxiety is ratcheted up, with the technology giving us so much more to be anxious about.

For what is the day's bill of fare on Blue Square but a long list of anxieties on which to ponder?

Across the universe, men are getting nervous about opportunities being lost, about missing a trick. They're looking at the market on a football match in Lithuania, at so many propositions, so many chances.

And it never stops.

This Olympics bullshit will be over in a few days and the fabulous multi-coloured presentations will vanish from the betting websites, and then we'll be on to the US Open tennis, and every day that tournament will offer us fifty ways to feel better for a little while.

So punters, with their complex array of anxieties, are not entirely unlike the Anti-Happiness League, whose motivation has long been defined as 'the fear that someone, somewhere, might be having a good time'. Likewise, punters are equally afraid that something, somewhere, will get away from them, that they will miss some astounding bit of 'value', that the world will somehow go on without them.

And here the money-merchants to whom Will Buckley referred are ready to enter the arena. Because every step of the way, you will pay for your anxiety. You will pay to start, and you will pay to stop. You will pay to indulge, you will pay when it all goes against you, and at the other end you will pay to recover what you can from the wreckage.

But that is the genius of capitalism – there is always money to be made by someone.

Just think . . . Like most other internet activities, internet gambling is currently banned in China. But here is a land where the old totalitarian boredom and the new capitalist anxiety are combusting. Maybe this gambling thing will be the ultimate challenge for them on the road to hegemony.

Can they figure out a way to let it happen? Can they let this hydra-headed monster out and let it roam? Can they somehow arrange to send the losers to a 12-step programme rather than the firing squad?

Certainly, they will have considered the money to be made, the astronomical numbers. Against this, they are old hands at considering the 'social consequences'. Which are also astronomical.

With the confidence of a nation which is about to rule the world for a thousand years, they will weigh it up in all its aspects . . . from every angle . . . and they will say no, nay, never . . . never in a thousand years, in ten thousand years, never in a million years.

To be sure, I have been very wrong about China, but this I know for sure: they will allow Amnesty International to open a suite of plush offices in the Forbidden City itself, Access All Areas, before they will give the green light to Paddy Power to do his thing.

All this free-booting individualism is apparently being encouraged in the new China. But there is something about gambling, especially the unsupervised online variety, that is just a bit too individualistic and a bit too free-booting. Especially for a race of people with a weakness for it.

A strong weakness, as we say.

One suspects that if the Chinese were simply allowed to do what they want in this situation, after so many decades of denial, we could be looking at scenes of chaos on an unprecedented scale. So I figure the ruling class will be keeping a lid on this for now, and for the foreseeable future.

You can take that to the bank.

A Bit of Previous
'A HAPPY DEATH' IN A PUB IN KILMACUD

WHEN I'VE SPOKEN to my friends about this thing that I'm writing, at some point in the conversation several of them have mentioned someone they know who gambles and who has taken a pretty big hit.

Yesterday a journalist friend referred to some guy he knows who lost fifteen grand recently. I've heard of a guy who had to cancel his wedding because he'd inadvertently lost about twenty grand that was supposed to pay for it. And I'm familiar with the case of a guy in County Roscommon who has been resolutely losing a long-established family grocery business, betting every day on anything that moves on the TV screen.

Everyone in Ireland seems to know someone who has lost a five-figure sum gambling, just as everyone in Ireland used to know someone who'd had an abortion. Yes, there is always someone who is worse off than yourself.

As I struggle to comprehend a mere four-figure deficit, and at the lower end of the four-figure spectrum too, with every chance of redemption, I think of these poor devils.

And I start to 'take the positives' out of it, as we sportsmen say.

• What I have lost so far is roughly the price of a decent television, with surround sound. On special offer.

- I don't drink and I don't smoke. As everyday vices go, this one is comparatively cheap.

- If I win it back, everything will be all right. In fact this is another of the ways in which gambling is a bit special – if you do it right, and actually make money at it, nobody gives a damn, even if you are theoretically addicted.

- If I were a Mormon, I'd have donated far more as a percentage of my salary just to pursue my religion.

To which the therapist would reply that in 'taking the positives' I am 'rationalizing' it, that I am using mere words to give myself a false impression, and to keep betting.

Words, words, words, the therapist would say disdainfully. Words are nothing, it is all about feelings.

But I reject this, especially when you consider that the addiction industry has virtually created its own language, full of words, words, words to which it gives a new meaning which suits its own purposes – words like 'recovery' and 'intervention', and these madly restrictive definitions of what constitutes a 'binge', so that eventually everyone who has two drinks in a row will be categorized as a binge drinker in need of a six-week course of residential treatment.

I also suspect that there's a gender bias involved in this rejection of the rational, which is stereotypically male, and the elevation of feelings, which are stereotypically female.

And I take it personally when I hear these people

denigrating words, words, words, because I know something about words. I make my living out of words, and I can assure these people that words are not mere objects that the mind produces in the absence of feelings, they are not 'mere' in any way.

Words, to anyone who cares about them, are intimately connected to feelings. The great writers convey the workings of the human heart with words, and nothing but words, and they do it an awful lot better than some shrink recycling the jargon of his trade.

And this leads me to a broader perspective on where I stand in relation to Luck.

Because I am fantastically lucky to be able to make my living out of words.

Do I appreciate it enough?

Mostly, none of us properly appreciates all the things that need to go right just to get us through the day, and to make it through the night. Like that little Italian, who had no idea how close his son came to death, there are probably things that have gone spectacularly right for us that we don't even know about.

But I'm stating my appreciation here anyway, perhaps as a way of touching wood, of registering my amazement that I have been so lucky to be able to make a living out of words.

And it has to be said that I got lucky mainly as a result of an outrageous gamble, the sort of gamble that in retrospect seems so wild, so deeply irresponsible, that even now, knowing that it all turned out fine, if I could go back there and do it again I probably wouldn't.

Essentially, one day back in 1979 or thereabouts, when I was eighteen years old, I sat in the office of *Hot Press* editor Niall Stokes, with two career choices in front of me: on the one side, I could continue my studies in UCD, at the end of which I would almost certainly become a rich lawyer; and on the other side, based on various pieces which the *Hot Press* had published, there was the opportunity to work full time for a rock'n'roll magazine that had almost no chance of surviving for any significant length of time. Not only that, but there was very little prospect that anyone who worked there could find alternative employment in the Irish media of that time – the newspapers had not yet recognized the existence of rock'n'roll, and RTE didn't seem like the most welcoming establishment either for tramps like us.

Against this, I had come to hate the idea of becoming a solicitor or a barrister, spending the rest of my working days in the company of folk who even at the age of eighteen were giving dinner parties.

If I could somehow have figured out a way to be as rich as a lawyer without having to do any of the appalling things that lawyers do I would gladly have submitted myself to that abysmal trade. But I just couldn't see it, at the time.

I knew that Frank O'Neill and his Armagh buddies seemed to spend most of their lives going to race meetings, but I figured it had taken them thirty years of remorseless lawyering to get there. And my attitude was also no doubt coloured by all the books I

was reading, books by Franz Kafka and Albert Camus
and Jean-Paul Sartre. *Nausea* by Sartre had a big
influence on me, and I can still recall sitting in a pub
in Kilmacud drinking steadily while enjoying Camus'
A Happy Death in one sitting. The perfect holiday
read there.

I still marvel at the pure madness of youth, which
made me reject the option which almost guaranteed
me a load of money for the rest of my life in favour
of a gig in an industry which hardly existed at all, in
any practical sense.

It was like running away to the circus, except that
the circus is an ancient occupation, with venerable
brand names and a well-established infrastructure.
By contrast, in Ireland at that time there were
approximately three recording studios, and it was still
a wondrous thing to receive a visit from an
international artiste other than Demis Roussos or
James Last.

Having made that call, I had to get a train down to
Athlone to tell my mother and father that I was
about to defy their reasonable expectations, that I
wasn't after all going to become a man of the law, a
highly respected member of the community, because
instead I was running away to this circus, which
wasn't even Duffy's circus, or Fossett's, just some
outfit they'd never heard of, a fly-by-night operation.

I am still somewhat surprised, even taken aback,
that they didn't simply shoot me on principle –
perhaps they were just in shock. Probably they were
just good people with a deeper understanding of
life's strangeness than I had realized, and I with a

lunatic light in my eye which made them acknowledge that resistance was futile. The light that can only come from a soul who has read *A Happy Death* in one sitting in a pub in Kilmacud, and felt that Camus was talking a barrel of sense there.

I wish that I could portray myself as the guy taking this massive gamble in a devil-may-care spirit, but in truth it was only much later that I understood the dimensions of the thing, how the entire course of my life was riding on this one call, as I sat in Niall Stokes' office.

I wish it had been a wild throw of the dice, but it was probably even more disturbing than that – because in truth, the dilemma I faced was no dilemma at all. I had no real sense of what I might be giving up as a rich lawyer. I had succumbed to a sort of temporary insanity, which had switched off the part of my brain that recognizes material self-interest.

In retrospect I can only compare it to that mythical first-time punter who wanders into a betting office knowing nothing of that world or of any better world, and who wins anyway, precisely because he knows nothing and understands nothing.

At least I'm pretty sure that I won that bet, the biggest bet of my life.

Then again, if I had learned to love the law, and to live with the dinner-party crowd, perhaps I would now be a big country solicitor and auctioneer with five cars and fourteen houses, or even President of the Law Reform Commission or even . . . no, I don't think so.

I think that whichever way you look at it, I won

that bet. I am the man who had all the luck on that day.

Before I sat down with Niall, I sat for a while in the National Gallery, which was near the *Hot Press* offices in Lower Mount Street. Looking at the big pictures, I wondered if I could be so lucky as to be able to work at something which gave me a voice, which might even enable me some day to write a book, maybe even that highest of all things, a novel which had some merit.

Yes, I have been a lucky so-and-so, in so many ways. I am fantastically lucky in my wife and my children, in where I live and in what I do.

I am lucky to be alive after drinking for so many years, during which several of my friends and acquaintances died young.

I am lucky that I got out of the drinking game when I did, in my mid-thirties, and that it gave me what I needed to write *The Rooms*, which couldn't have been written otherwise – yes, even when I have ventured into the badlands of addiction, I have been lucky.

And I realize that these statements of my good fortune may be the prelude to my getting knocked down by the proverbial bus, but even if that happens, during my last moments on this earth, as my life flashes before me, I would have to concede that on the whole, when you add it all up, more often than not I have been a lucky so-and-so.

So why the fuck can't I back a few more winners?

I guess that in their way, the gods are being kind to me here too. Because I have indeed been horribly unlucky sometimes, but then if my share of bad luck is being doled out in this way I should probably be grateful for that too.

Given all that has gone right for me in real life, it may even be morally wrong to expect anything resembling a fair shake in my sporting life. So when Turkey cost me that monkey at Euro 2008 in such a grotesque fashion, perhaps the gods were sending me this message: with all the blessings we have bestowed upon you, still you come to us expecting more? Still you want to push your luck?

When Garcia put it in the water on the sixteenth at Oakland Hills, perhaps the gods were sending me this message: each morning you wake up and you are living in paradise, and you want free money on top of that? You want another 300 quid just for watching golf? You think 300 quid is a fair payment for watching Sergio trying not to blow it again, live on Sky Sports? Sorry, kid, there are men in this world with actual problems.

And in thwarting all my most valiant efforts, these same mysterious forces are reminding me just how hard it is to find favour with the gods.

It makes me wonder why even the most fortunate of men keep looking for more and more, looking for free money when they have no need for money at all, pushing their luck way beyond the limit, until they create this hellish other world for themselves in which they are tormented by events over which they have no control.

So tormented, in fact, it eats away at their good fortune until eventually there is nothing left, and no way back.

I guess it's just the way men are, unable to give in to their human weakness, to admit that they are licked, even the smartest of them. Because if we know nothing else about addiction, about life itself, we know this: smart people do stupid things.

All the time.

24 August 2008

Deposit: 100

Day after day the rains came, in the aftermath of the Beijing massacre. And I languished in the slough of despond.

I could find no way to shift that rock. No winner could I find without a loser close behind, draining another hundred and another, until I found myself again with the gambler's amnesia – the old gamnesia. A bad place to be, though mercifully one from which I have emerged in the past with a new surge of punting energy, a new way of winning – for a while, at least.

And by way of black comedy, I note that for a while there on Betfair you could back Hillary Clinton at 47/1 to be President of the United States – not in 2012, but this time around. Since the only hope she has of becoming President this time around is if Barack Obama is assassinated, this means that there is now effectively a market on the assassination of Barack Obama. By taking a bit of that 47/1 about Hillary, you are implicitly having a double, on Obama getting shot and Hillary to beat McCain.

Indeed some of us wondered when we'd be able to bet on the outcome of murder trials and other such sombre events which are supposedly outside the sporting realm, and now we realize that the first step on this journey has been taken, albeit furtively.

There is darkness visible, too, in Sky Sports' indefatigable pursuit of women. Illustrating the advertising slogan that 'it matters more when there's money on it', there's now a woman clearly in a state of high excitement as she watches in slow motion the climactic moment of some ball game, her expression one of ecstasy as she gets the right result.

In another version, she is following the action with a man, presumably her husband, as if this thing of ours were now a normal form of recreation for the respectable middle-class couple, a big night in, betting on the live dog racing at Walthamstow. As he savours the sweet moment of victory she watches him admiringly. By picking the winner, he has demonstrated again that he is a man. A smart man. A shrewd man. A man in control.

Christ, they never give up, do they?

And I must not give up either. Not now, while there is still time . . .

I may be giving up soon enough, but for now I have made a vow to see it through until Valhalla. And by God, that is what I will do. After all, I have always believed that in order to give up something, first of all you must do a lot of it.

I did not give up smoking, for example, by gradually reducing my daily intake. In fact I did the opposite, smoking my head off until it was bringing me no pleasure at all – how could it? On any given day, there was hardly any time when I was not smoking, so there was nothing against which my smoking satisfaction could be measured.

People don't stop drinking either by winding it down in leisurely fashion but by ramping it up until they are completely destroyed.

No doubt it is much of a muchness with the gambling.

And for me, with only a few weeks left of this quest, there's not much point in giving up, even if it is the right thing to do.

But what I need, to get that rock up the hill again, is some fresh way of addressing the ancient challenge, something that gets the old juices going. I think that what I need now is a plan. Or at least a better plan than all the other plans.

The one that appeals to me the most, at the end of this wicked month, goes something like this: I am . . . a cricketer. Like I said, through online betting I have fallen in love with the game of cricket, which is a boon.

I note that the Indian Cricket League on satellite TV is sponsored by a firm of solicitors which specializes in compensation claims. It is their proud boast that they are 'the future of claiming'. Interesting, too, that for some weird reason they feel that the people they want to reach with their advertising are the sort of people who might be watching the cricket on TV, perhaps having a small wager on the side, and thoughts of free money.

I know how they feel.

And now I see myself as . . . a batsman . . . who comes to the crease with about seven wickets down, needing to construct an innings. Needing runs, lots of runs. A really good knock, as they say.

In actual money terms, the plan is to turn this latest deposit of 100 – the last one? – into something that will give me a fighting fund for Valhalla. And at this stage I should probably reveal that I will be backing America to win the Ryder Cup.

I will 'leave that with you', as they say, and I will deal with it in more detail as the great day approaches. But until then I have work to do, out in the middle. I have a wicket to protect, and I need to start scoring.

In fact I have a score in mind. Starting with this 100 (my 'wicket', as it were), to reach 500 or anything in that region is acceptable. And then, high on the improbability of it all, I will be putting the lot on America to win the Ryder Cup. That is the plan, anyway, the equivalent of the batsman hitting it out of the ground to win the game with the last ball. Or if not actually to win, at least to get out without losing much – which is, as we now know, the Grail.

Let us go then, you and I, on this, our last journey. Let us see what we will find at the end of this deeply felt meditation on memory and loss.

And let us take this as our motto: Urgency Without Indiscretion.

This is the motto of the wise batsman, as he seeks to construct a major innings – Urgency Without Indiscretion.

Urgency, of course, is essential, because we are in grave jeopardy here. But indiscretion is forbidden, because if you lose your wicket in a moment of indiscretion, all will be lost.

Even if you have rolled that proverbial rock to within spitting distance of the pinnacle, with just one moment of indiscretion you are walking away despondently, a beaten man. Because somehow you have crossed that line from urgency into indiscretion, so great was your need.

You tried to hit it for four or even six, when you should have just nurdled it away for one, or refused it altogether.

Of course the batsman needs to accelerate, needs to time his innings. If he just nurdles away all day, his wicket may remain intact, but he won't get enough runs. And if he accelerates in the wrong place at the wrong time, he'll be back in the shed.

Let us go then, one more time . . .

SCORE – 100

⚽ 50 on Chelsea to beat Wigan @ 2/5 – **Win**
A couple of runs on the board.   120

▬ 120 on Chicago Cubs to beat Washington @ 1/4 – **Win**
Couldn't refuse that one.   145

⚽ 50 on Man Utd to beat Portsmouth @ 3/4 – **Win**
At that price, I might have tried for a boundary.
But I'm still 'playing myself in'.   190

🎾 45 on Hantuchova to beat Groenefeld @ 4/9 – **Lose**
We are often accused of not understanding women.
What is increasingly clear is that we don't understand
women's tennis.   145

🎾 145 on Safin to beat Spadea @ 2/7 – **Win**
A positive reply.   185

🎾 85 on De Los Rios to beat Sromova @ 8/15 – **Win**
I try that shot again, on the women's tennis,
with Rosanna De Los Rios. It's a boundary.   230

Ⓜ 130 on Sri Lanka to beat India @ 4/9 – **Lose**
My first indiscretion, a wild swipe on Sri Lanka.
So the first serious threat to my 'wicket' comes in the
game of cricket. Another of those ironies by which great
saints are made.   100

Free Money

● 100 on Gulbis to beat Johansson @ 2/9 – **Win**
At this US Open, I'm getting the feeling that 'my eye is in'. 125

𝕸 90 on Sri Lanka to beat India @ 4/7 – **Win**
A welcome return to form. Another boundary. 170

● 100 on Jankovic to beat Zheng @1/4 – **Win**
Keeping the scoreboard ticking over. 195

● 60 on Gonzalez to beat Niemenen @ 1/3 – **Win**
More runs on the board. 215

𝕸 60 on South Africa to beat England @ 5/6 – **Lose**
Another setback on the cricket pitch. Oh the irony. 155

● 125 on Groenefeld to beat Moore @ 2/9 – **Win**
A decent response. 185

● 70 on Karlovic to beat Querrey @ 4/6 – **Lose**
An ugly scene. 115

● 65 on Seppi to beat Garcia-Lopez @ 4/11 – **Win**
Nurdling away. 140

● 130 on Murray to beat Melzer @ 1/6 – **Win**
A five-set 'thriller'. But Murray keeps me going. 165

⚽ 70 on Kerry to beat Cork @ 4/11 – **Win**
Tempted to hit it out of the ground. Settled for the single. 190

45 on Del Potro to beat Simon @ 1/2 – **Win**
Runs on the board.   215

110 on Safina to beat Groenefeld @ 1/4 – **Win**
So we know nothing about women?   240

40 on Mauresmo to beat Pennetta @ 8/15 – **Lose**
Evidently not.   200

50 on Mike Weir to win Deutsche Bank tournament
@ 4/5 in-running – **Lose**
Indiscretion.   150

145 on Vijay Singh to win Deutsche Bank tournament
@ 1/4 in-running – **Win**
Urgency.   185

90 on Boston to beat Baltimore @ 4/9 – **Win**
Still don't know the rules of that game.
It doesn't seem to matter.   230

70 on Jankovic to beat Bammer @ 1/7 – **Win**
Keeping the scoreboard ticking over.   240

80 on Djokovic to beat Robredo @ 1/8 – **Win**
Still ticking. Albeit after a five-set 'thriller'.   250

75 on Safina to beat Pennetta @ 1/5 – **Win**
Too easy.   265

Free Money

⚫ 60 on S. Williams to beat V. Williams @ 4/6 – **Win**
Yes, my eye is in. 305

⚫ 90 on Djokovic to beat Roddick @ 8/13 – **Win**
I said to my wife, 'Djokovic or Roddick?'
She thought about it, and she said 'Djokovic'.
They all count. 365

⚫ 35 on Safina to beat S. Williams @ 2/1 – **Lose**
A small setback, worth a shot. 330

╎ 40 on McIlroy to win Swiss Open @ 11/8 in-running – **Lose**
Rory (19) bogeyed the last and was beaten in a play-off during
which he missed a putt which was allegedly 18 inches
but which looked to me more like 12 inches.
He'll be back. And so will I. 290

⚫ 180 on Murray to beat Nadal @ 8/13 in-running – **Win**
I said to my wife, 'Murray or Nadal?'
She thought about it, and she said, 'Murray'.
It is a massive call. Andy comes down the track and
hits it out of the ground. 400

⚫ 75 on Federer to beat Murray @ 4/9 – **Win**
The heart says Murray, the head says Federer.
The head wins, so does The Fed. 430

⚫ 25 on Mathieu to beat Navarro @ 4/9 – **Lose**
French surrender monkey. 405

60 on Milwaukee Brewers to beat Cincinnati @ 1/3 – **Win**
What made Milwaukee famous, made a loser out of me.
But not this time.   425

60 on Petrova to beat Garbin @ 1/6 – **Win**
Ticking over.   435

30 on Minnesota to beat Kansas City @ 1/3 – **Lose**
A rare loss at baseball.   405

80 on Wigan to beat Bradford @ 4/7 – **Win**
A sweet shot. A boundary.   450

100 on Sussex to beat Middlesex @ 2/7 in-running – **Win**
More runs.   480

25 on Chelsea to beat Man City @ 5/6 – **Win**
'A good knock,' as they say.   500

An exemplary knock indeed, and now I think it is time to play the big shot.

I am 500 not out, and at this stage they'd be standing up in the pavilion, applauding me, a well-deserved tribute which I acknowledge graciously with a wave of the bat. And they'd probably agree that there's not much point in risking my wicket any more, looking for singles and twos, when I have so many runs on the board, and that one big shot still in the locker.

That one big shot . . .

I have had many winners in these last few days, visualizing myself as a cricketer at the crease, so if I had taken that one big shot on Chelsea to beat Man City, or had a truly massive punt on The Fed to beat Murray in the final of the US Open, a tennis tournament at which I had at last found a run of form . . . then again, if I had 'gone for it' on Mauresmo or Hantuchova . . .

I held my discipline and kept my shape, knowing that if I had gone for the big shot during this phase, I would somehow, inexplicably, in some way that maddeningly surpasses all understanding, have been drawn towards the wrong play, towards Mauresmo and not Federer, towards Minnesota and not Milwaukee. I know this, though I could never begin to explain it to myself or to anyone else. Because even as I savour these moments out in the middle, I am venturing back towards the land of Sisyphus.

Four times now, four times I have gone for that one big shot, only to be skittled by Woods and Karlsson, Croatia and America. I swung at the four of them, and missed. And if I had just nurdled them away or played a straight bat, I would now have such a huge profit percentage, they would be studying my methods in the more advanced academies of punting – indeed I would hope that they will be doing that anyway, factoring in the 'acts of God' that have left me here making this last brave stand.

Of course they should be studying this document on the other side of the wall, in the mental institutions and the addiction-treatment centres. But they already have their holy books. And in this one there is too much questioning of the very fundamentals of their belief-system.

And to be perfectly truthful, if I wasn't engaged in this process, compiling this journal, I don't know if I would be indulging in those big plays, which have scuppered all my savings and wise investments. I just don't know if I would simply be walking away now in a new pair of shoes, if I didn't have this narrative to sustain. It is possible that without the heightened reality of this project, I would now have four new pairs of shoes, made of the finest Italian leather.

But then, even when I was blowing my wad I figured there was something inherently more interesting in that journey than in the more wholesome tale of a man withdrawing his winnings and going to the shoe shop – even if it was a very good shoe shop, and the shoes were very expensive.

So as I put that hard-earned monkey on America to win the Ryder Cup, I am affirming that this is indeed a quest for the Grail, not a quest for shoes.

And of course, since you are reading this several months after I've written it, you already know how it all turned out. Knowing the result, you may even be laughing at me now, as I proceed with the build-up to this last big play, backing America again, America who let me down so horribly in Beijing.

Backing America, in the week that Lehman Brothers goes wallop, Merrill Lynch is sold off for thirty bob and AIG is bailed out by Joe Six-Pack and really, the whole damn thing is going down, down, down.

Backing America, in the week that candidate McCain called Wall Street 'a casino' – a good call there from McCainsy, who himself is allegedly partial to a punt. Good call, but in fairness I think I got there before him.

Backing America . . .

A MOMENT OF SOBER REFLECTION
SCENES OF CHAOS ON AN
UNPRECEDENTED SCALE

FREE MONEY, they say, was at the root of it. Interest rates were reduced to such low levels, you could borrow money virtually for free, which meant that banks felt the need to get into the bullshit business in a serious way if they wanted to make serious money. As if, otherwise, they would never have been tempted into the twilight zone of 'sub-prime'. As if their greed was dormant until they were faced with the challenge of free money.

Greed, I believe, is a bit like cholesterol. There is good cholesterol and bad cholesterol, there is good greed and bad greed. The good stuff can be a great motivator. The bad stuff can kill you.

Gordon Gekko thought it was all good, but of course it is not. Because it is abundantly clear now that there is this thing called bad greed, which is not only fatal to those who have it, it is destroying our world.

So McCain was in the right neighbourhood when he referred to Wall Street as a casino, but in truth he is doing an injustice to the casino operators of North America. Compared to their corporate brethren, those men in Las Vegas and Atlantic City have been running an honest and wholesome enterprise, which creates employment and provides much harmless and even life-affirming pleasure to the common man.

There will never be a better time to raise the question of how America can justify the banning of online gambling, at least of the sporting variety. There are many forms of online gambling that have been permitted to flourish wildly on Wall Street, resulting in scenes of chaos on an unprecedented scale. So how is it possible that a man is barred from sitting at his computer and having ten dollars on the Kentucky Derby, but he is perfectly free to sit at the same computer and have a punt that makes somebody else's pension fund disappear?

I do not know the answer to that.

I suspect there is no answer to that.

And now for the first time since 1929 they have banned the stock-market practice of 'short-selling', which is another word for betting, which is another word for losing just now.

But there are indications that the effects of the corporate contagion are being felt in the more respectable environs of sports betting. I am told that these days, even in Ireland, the punters in the offices are thinking a bit harder before they have a bet – no harm in that – and that when they do bet, they are reducing their stakes.

For a while there, 50 quid had become the new 20 quid, and 100 had become the new 50. Now, anecdotal evidence suggests that the process is being reversed, with 50 the new 100, and 20 the new 50. And they are saying that the average online stake is getting smaller.

But as I walk down the main street of Arklow, even if every other shop is closing down, buggered out of existence by the recession, I know that there are some that will remain.

The Bear Stearnses and Lehman Brothers and Northern Rocks of this world may come and go, but Paddy Power won't need to be rescued any time soon.

And hell, even I am better than those Wall Street guys. In a volatile market, it seems that I have managed my portfolio far more prudently than the big-swinging-mickey brigade. Yes, it is fair to say that by all the key indicators, Declan Lynch has been outperforming Merrill Lynch by a considerable margin.

Sure, I'm a bit behind, but goddammit I am way ahead of those boys. The taxpayer won't have to rescue me, at least not this week. And probably not next week either.

In fact over the next few days America can pump a load of liquidity into my system by winning the Ryder Cup and leaving me virtually debt-free.

America . . .

18 September 2008

⚑ 500 on America @ 6/5 to win the Ryder Cup

And why America?

Well, I guess I have fancied them to win this Ryder Cup from way back, just like from way back I fancied China to win the most gold medals.

Indeed . . .

Then again, I spoke to a man last week, a golf professional whose knowledge of the game is unrivalled, and he stated with chilling confidence that Europe would win. The aficionado feels that Europe is 'a well-balanced side'. At which point I moved him on to another topic, so dispirited was I by his certitude.

I cannot desert America now, after all we've been through. Even though it is perfectly possible that I am on the wrong side of history here, the point at which America lost its mojo, every which way, and never got it back. Maybe we're at that point right now, or maybe America is about to get its mojo back in a big way at Valhalla.

This is the size of it.

Valhalla, which is in Louisville, Kentucky, birthplace of my favourite writer, Hunter S. Thompson – is there some good ju-ju in that?

I confess that I have found the recent European triumphs vaguely revolting, with all these guys who couldn't win a major between them playing like heroes when they've got eleven other guys along with them.

They're all heroes now, baby!

Though since the orgy at the K Club, my man Padraig

Harrington, in fairness, has done it all by himself, three times. Which only leaves eleven of them playing like God, routinely rattling in the putts from 60 feet with their eyes closed, when they've got all their mates along with them – chokers to a man when they're on their own out there, facing the back nine on Sunday in a major, alone, all alone.

My distaste was doubtless more keenly felt because I backed America at the K Club, though I would remind you that I had 80 quid on them, whereas our old friend Mr Graham Calvert had 347,000 quid on them.

Remember that?

My stake has risen in the meantime from 80 to 500, but unlike some of the more vulnerable investors, I don't see a Calvert-like progression whereby I'll be having 3,000 on the next one, at Celtic Manor, and then 20,000 . . .

Again I would remind you that my name is Declan, not Merrill Lynch.

So a monkey it is, on America, probably the last of the monkeys in this part of the world. As to what Mr Calvert will be investing this year, we will draw a discreet veil.

But I am heartened by reports which suggest that Captain Faldo sees himself as something of a rocker, installing a drum kit in the locker room at Valhalla for reasons best known to himself and his great mate Phil Collins, perhaps because he wrongly believes that guys like him and Ian Poulter are embodying the spirit of rock'n'roll in an otherwise stuffy old place. To this end, reportedly, he has also included in his entourage the DJ Spoony.

Frankly, you've gotta be betting against those guys.

22 September 2008 – Break-even-or-as-near-as-makes-no-difference

It is the morning after Valhalla and my journey is complete. I am resting now, after a remarkable triumph.

In the mind's eye, I see the defining moments, and I euphorically recall them . . . Stricker holing a 15-footer on the eighteenth for a crucial half . . . Kim making Garcia putt from less than 2 feet, and Garcia missing . . . Casey duffing a bunker shot when he had Mahan under the gun, and then Mahan holing a crazy one on the seventeenth that would otherwise have gone 15 feet past . . . Furyk getting it done against Jiménez.

And all this without my man Tiger, still resting up.

I am enjoying too the perfect symmetry of Team USA winning back the 600 that Team USA lost me in Beijing, just as Tiger won back the 400 he lost me at Augusta. Some might say that this indicates there is a sort of justice in the world, that it all evens up in the end.

Which it doesn't, really.

Because even as we reach out for the Grail, we know that it will always remain strangely elusive, or that we will grasp it only to find that it has turned to nothing in our hands, that it is a trick of the light.

I am at break-even-or-as-near-as-makes-no-difference, which is not break-even precisely. But after all we've been through, 100 here or there is what the pollsters would term 'within the margin of error'. Throw in a few hundred more which got away from me out there, and you can see how hard it is to balance the old books.

Though as we know, the purpose of gambling is not necessarily to be counting your money, the purpose of gambling is gambling.

We also know by now that it is not a fair fight.

Remarkably, in turning that 100 into 1,100 by visualizing myself as a batsman at the crease, I have had thirty winners – twenty-nine small winners, and one big winner. Against this, I have had ten losers.

A pretty sobering ratio there, which shows us what we are up against, even when we manage to devise a plan which works for us, and which we follow unwaveringly.

This is how hard it is, at a time when a multitude of innocents are discovering the pleasures of gambling. Dear God, there was even a project in the Young Scientists Exhibition last year about the mathematics of gambling – which was very interesting, I'm sure, though if you're doing the maths maybe the most important number to bear in mind is that half of all the new entrants on the *Sunday Times* Rich List have made their fortunes out of internet gambling or casinos.

For them too, in a twisted way, this is not an unhappy ending. Because I have demonstrated that there is hope.

Epilogue

A few days later I won a hundred on Lorena Ochoa, which is not a lot, in the context of my overall losses on the great Mexican, or in relation to the situation at Goldman Sachs, but it suggests again that if you stick with the blue-chip investments, over time they will reward you – it's like what they used to say about the stock market, except in this case it might be vaguely true.

Again it might give the impression that gambling, in the long term, is swings and roundabouts – you lose on Tiger, you eventually get it back, you lose on America, you eventually get it back; Ochoa wins a few, loses a few, then starts winning again.

Again this would suggest that there is hope, and as William Bolitho observed, a gambler is nothing but a man who makes his living out of hope.

Ah, but as we have also observed many times, it is a double-edged thing, this hope. In fact it is so dangerous that when I look at it now, after all we've been through, I would say that hope should officially be registered by the United Nations as a disease.

And as for gambling itself, it gives me no pleasure to suggest that the same UN should long ago have declared it an epidemic that has every chance of becoming a pandemic.

I have tried to be Fair and Balanced. I have tried to be equally sceptical about the respective bullshit of the gambling industry and the anti-gambling industry, but I think I am reaching a moment now when I must come down on one side or the other, when I must 'call it', just like I would call a Monday evening match on Setanta in the Blue Square Premier League.

I think of a friend of mine, a well-known Irish rock'n'roll

musician, who was reminiscing one day about his life as a drinker and all the fun that he had had and all the good people he had met, until at the end it darkened and went bad on him, because there was just too much . . . and he paused as he sought the right word . . . there was just too much . . . destruction.

And that is what I am feeling now about the gambling.

The anti-gambling industry will feed you the most terrible bullshit, and for this it is to be reviled, and yet it is not the sort of bullshit that results in destruction. It is the sort of bullshit that results in defeat for many a decent man who is only trying to pick a few winners like his father before him, and it leads to a general dampening of the human spirit.

And I suppose there is destruction involved in that too, in the dead hand gaining the advantage. But for the gambler, there is always the risk of destruction on a somewhat different scale – the sort of destruction that ends up in a court of law in which the judge remarks that this is the fourteenth case of embezzlement that he has seen in the last two weeks, and by the way, what is this Danish women's handball?

This is the sort of destruction that leaves you losing everything and everyone and living on the side of the road. The sort of destruction which traditionally takes place in that locked room with the service revolver on the table. And a bottle of good whiskey. For luck.

Ah, luck . . . 'All of us have bad luck and good luck,' suggested Robert Collier, perhaps the original self-help guru, in *The Secret of the Ages*. 'The man who persists through the bad luck – who keeps right on going – is the man who is there when the good luck comes, and is ready for it.'

An uplifting statement there from old Collier, but you can carve those words on the tombstones of more than a few punters who kept right on going. Because sometimes, in the nature of things, it is just not possible to keep on going.

A few days after I finished this diary, for example, I was driving in to Arklow on a Sunday morning.

And for a few moments I knew for certain that I was going to die.

A car coming in the opposite direction had crossed over to my side of the road and was coming straight for me. I braked, knowing I was doomed. And in that mad instant of catastrophic clarity, about three seconds before impact, the other car swerved back to its own side of the road, and that was that.

I was still alive, not dead.

What were the odds on that?

It's hard to tell, because I don't know what was happening in the other car. Was he rooting around for a CD, taking his eye off the road? Was he coming from a wedding in Wexford, still pissed? Was he doing this for a laugh? Was he a she? In those out-of-body moments, when I knew I was about to die, I didn't get to see the driver, just the car.

And what if I had been a better driver, with Lewis Hamilton's reflexes? Possibly I would have executed some brilliant evasive move, swerving from my side of the road to the other side, which in the circumstances would have been exactly the wrong thing to do. And possibly, in that scenario, when they had found what was left of us in the wreckage, they would have blamed me for the accident – by the looks of it, it was I who was in the wrong lane.

So then my wife and children would have to live with this stigma which I had brought upon them with my bad driving. Perhaps the grief-maddened relatives of my 'victim' would seek some terrible revenge. Ah, luck . . . the things that happen, and the things that don't happen.

Merely by staying alive we are beating the odds in ways that we barely comprehend. It is only a near-death experience that makes us appreciate this. And when the shock of it fades away, we again regard our continuing existence as being perfectly normal, a mere platform from which to speculate and accumulate.

What is this deep insanity which tells us that we can predict things, that we can control them?

It is a question that is especially poignant at this time. Because when I started the diary, with that reference to the unfortunate Jérôme Kerviel losing billions at Société Générale, clearly I was seeing a parallel between the internet punter and the wizards of the financial services industry, in the sense that they are both essentially gambling. And though I followed that parallel line all the way through, I could never have predicted back in January that we would now be seeing Kerviel as some kind of a small-time loser.

Back then I was routinely referring to the Bradford & Bingley as if it were a permanent institution. I was so absorbed in trying to pick winners of football matches, I never for a moment contemplated the possibility that, by the end of the financial year, I myself might be running a more successful business than the Bradford & Bingley.

We know nothing. We do not know if we will be living or dying at the end of the day. Yet there is a sickness in our souls that compels us to carry on predicting, and to back our predictions with money, thinking that we won't be disappointed.

What is the difference between the guy who thinks he can influence the result of the Cup Final by sitting in a certain armchair superstitiously wearing odd socks, and the 'shrewdie' who has fifty grand ante-post on next year's St Leger?

The difference, I guess, is fifty grand. And not much more.

So I put my shoulder to that rock one more time, and I rolled it about three-quarters of the way up that hill. And even if I had heaved it all the way to the summit, in terms of money I would only have what I had in January before I set out on this quest.

All that concentration . . . all that work . . . all that time . . . all that winning and all that losing . . . and we're not even back where we started.

And we are the lucky ones.

But the luckiest ones are those who have somehow always known the truth of a line credited to the Renaissance man Girolamo Cardano. An Italian mathematician, physician, astrologer and gambler, he thought deeply enough about the plight of the punter to conceive a book about games of chance, *Liber Di Ludo Aleae*. Written in the 1560s, it contains the first systematic treatment of probability, and a helpful section on efficient cheating methods.

Cardano was such a shrewdie, it is thought that he invented the combination lock. And he was accused of heresy because he compiled and published a horoscope of Jesus Christ. He supposedly died on the exact day that he had predicted in his own astrological chart, though some suspected that he had committed suicide – another man afflicted with the punter's pathological need to be proved right.

Cardano, who in passing was the first man to describe typhoid fever – yes he would have been good on fever, good on the causes of fever – left this world in a better state than he found it, even if the manner of his leaving is still the subject of a steward's inquiry, as it were. But he left us with one line above all that may guide us to a better life:

'The greatest advantage in gambling,' he wrote, 'lies in not playing at all.'

Glossary

The odds are the price offered by the bookie, supposedly representing the chance that you have of winning. The odds are expressed by what normal people would know as a fraction, and it is important to note that the punter's stake is represented by the second part of the fraction: thus 2/1 (two to one 'against') means that if you have a bet of one euro, you will win two. Or if you like, if you have a bet of 1,000, you will win 2,000. And you will also get back your stake. Which makes some people think they've actually won three times what they staked. In fact this merely reveals their lack of self-esteem, this sense of surprise that they would actually get their own money back.

Likewise 1/2 (two to one 'on') means that you have to bet 2 euros to win one. Again you get your stake back if you win. You get nothing back if you lose.

When the first number is smaller than the second number, it is known as 'odds on', so at 1/2 your horse is 'an odds-on shot'. And an odds-on shot, in theory, is supposed to have a better chance than a horse which is 'odds-against'. In theory, a horse at 1/2 should comfortably beat a horse at 2/1. In practice, you will probably lose anyway.

And first-time punters can be seduced by the odds.

You might hear a radio disc jockey, for example, trying to raise money for charity by betting on races at Cheltenham. And he is 200 euros down, so he sees there's a horse at 20/1, and he says, 'If I put 10 euros on this I will win 200 and all our troubles will be over.'

Theoretically he is right. But there's a reason the horse is

20/1 – most likely, it is not a very good horse.

And most likely the disc jockey, yet again, will be wrong.

Three-star cast-iron plungers originally came to our attention in Flann O'Brien's great novel *At Swim-Two-Birds*. The main character receives racing tips through the post from one Verney Wright of Wyvern Cottage, Newmarket, Suffolk, and the best of these are described as three-star cast-iron plungers. These are almost certain to win, right up until the moment that they don't win, and then Verney has to compose another letter explaining where it all went wrong – dark forces usually have conspired to thwart him.

As for the term itself, its origin is uncertain but is probably related to the way a punter 'plunges' on a sure thing, casting aside all his cares in order to make a big splash. A plunger is also a device for clearing blocked pipes with a sucking action, just as the punter hopes to clean out the bookie.

The practice of punters sending money through the post to the likes of Verney and others who declare that they are 'in the know' is an ancient one. It appeals to the horse-player's sense of mystery, his belief that there is precious 'information' out there that can give him an edge. He rarely stops to wonder why, if Verney's information was so great, he'd be reduced to shaking down suckers in this way.

Shrewdies are thought to be more astute than the average punter. But then punters have a deep need to imagine that if they keep going in the right direction, they will eventually attain some higher wisdom which will bring them closer to the Grail – the shrewdies seem to possess this wisdom. So if they didn't exist, they would have to be invented by the average punter, as role models.

This mythical shrewdness can manifest itself in various ways. A particular shrewdie may be said to possess a mysterious expertise in the area of Scottish football, having spotted some pattern in the doings of Kilmarnock, East Fife and Brechin City – 'For six months he backed East Stirling playing away from home and bought a house out of it.'

Or he may just give the general impression that he is a man with a plan, a man who is not just doing this for the good of his health, a shrewd man indeed.

Only his bookmaker knows how shrewd the shrewdie really is. And he's not telling. But he seems to speak of him with some affection.

Betting in-running is a speciality of the online providers. It means that you can have a bet while an event is in progress, with the odds changing all the time, depending on how your selection is going.

It can be quite leisurely – you can have a bet on the second day of a four-day golf tournament. Or it can be insanely frenetic, with some providers 'pricing up' every point in a tennis match, or allowing you to bet on a horse race after it starts, and until it is physically impossible to bet any more.

Bookies are very fond of the 'in-running'. Which should tell you all you need to know.

Single bets, in which you bet on one thing at a time, to win, are the ones overwhelmingly favoured here. But there are such things as **Doubles**, which involve making two selections. If the first one wins, your winnings plus the original stake are placed on the second selection. So it is very nice if your double 'comes up', but if the first one wins and the second one loses, you get nothing. A **Treble** operates on the same principle, except with three selections, all of which must win.

Then you're looking at **Trixies**, **Trifectas**, **Accumulators**, **Yankees**, **Fourfolds**, **Penfolds**, **Patents**, **Heinzes**, **Super-heinzes**, **Lucky Fifteens**, and something called a **Goliath**.

You don't want to know what these things are.

You really don't.

A monkey is betting slang for 500 pounds, or 500 euros, or 500 of anything that the punter is investing. It would seem just as easy to say '500' as to say 'a monkey', but perhaps the punter wishes to raise his sights above the raw numbers. If you find yourself having a lot of 'monkeys', it is only a matter of time until you also find yourself sitting at a table in Las Vegas next to a man who is wearing a large green floppy hat.

It should also be noted that the standard six-week residential course in an addiction treatment centre, at current rates, will cost you about twelve monkeys.

Value is a strange thing. The punter is looking for 'value' in the same way as the mythical housewife is looking for value at the January sales – it involves assessing the market and getting something at a price that is better than it ought to be. This makes the punter feel good about himself, and the 'edge' it has given him.

But there is one small difference between the punter and the shopper. Even when the punter gets 'value', he may still walk away with a considerable loss. In fact the 'value' on offer may have diverted him away from the more likely winner, which was not available at such a competitive price. Still, he consoles himself with the thought that, even though he lost all his money, he still got the 'value'. He realizes that for the mythical housewife, this is an elusive concept.

Laying is what the bookie does. But the arrival of the online betting exchanges such as Betfair has made it possible for the punter to take bets from other punters, to start 'laying'. Essentially this means hoping that something will lose. Which is a novelty, and which, on the face of it, might seem easier than hoping something will win.

It eventually becomes apparent that it's actually just as hard for the amateur to make money by 'laying' as by betting normally. In some cases it can take several days to understand this; mostly it takes about twenty minutes.

Laying off is what the bookie does when he is exposed to potentially large losses, and he covers himself by betting on the same proposition with other bookies, ideally to leave himself with a small profit whatever happens. Alternatively he can take the bet, take a gamble and hope for the best.

But generally, he didn't get to where he is today by gambling.

Draw No Bet is a popular online betting product whereby if the match finishes in a draw, you get your money back. To compensate the bookie for his generosity, if you back the winner, the odds are greatly reduced. For many punters, getting their money back feels the same as winning.

Virtual Racing is pretend racing featuring pretend horses or pretend dogs with made-up names, 'running' at pretend tracks. The odds are calculated by a system which allegedly ensures that a 2/1 shot has exactly a 2/1 chance, mathematically. Many punters now prefer this to actual racing.

Fun bets are an advertising concept dreamed up by the 'gaming' industry to make itself look normal and respectable. They rely on the co-operation of a compliant media who unfailingly publicize these 'fun bets', who think it's hilarious that odds are being offered on, say, Dustin the Turkey to be the next manager of the Republic of Ireland football team, or Michael O'Leary to be the next Pope.

Oh, how they laugh!

The NFL, otherwise known as **American Football**, is understood by almost nobody outside of North America, yet it is shown on Sky Sports late on Sunday night. Which means that it attracts a large audience of European punters who have not the faintest idea what is happening on the field, but who bet on it anyway, because it's the end of the weekend, the last stop on the line. When all seems to be lost, they are drawn inexorably to the NFL, or the 'gridiron', hoping against hope that the Green Bay Packers will get them out of a hole – though they know not whether the Green Bay Packers are from a place called Green Bay, or a place called Packers.

By the early hours of Monday morning, nobody really cares.

Unusual betting patterns is a diplomatic term used by spokesmen for the 'gaming' industry when they're describing a massive scam which is perpetrated against them, or which they have foiled before it could be perpetrated. For example, if a tennis player loses the first set 0–6, and is seen to be limping horribly, vomiting and receiving oxygen, and still the money keeps pouring on him, this is an unusual betting pattern which suggests that he is about to make an amazing recovery, and win the match. Which is invariably what he does.

All betting patterns which emanate from anywhere in the former Soviet Union are assumed to be unusual.

Gamble Responsibly is a slogan used widely by official agencies to encourage punters to go easy. It is a contradiction in terms.

Gamblers Anonymous is a fellowship for people with a desire to stop gambling. It is free of charge.

It works.